LIVE NUDE ELF:
THE SEXPERIMENTS OF REVEREND JEN

LIVE NUDE ELF:
THE SEXPERIMENTS
OF REVEREND JEN

REVEREND JEN

SOFT SKULL PRESS
BROOKLYN

Library of Congress Cataloging-in-Publication Data is available.

ISBN (13) 978-1-59376-244-5

Cover design by David Janik
Interior design by Maria E. Torres, Neuwirth & Associates, Inc.
Printed in the United States of America

Soft Skull Press
An Imprint of Counterpoint LLC
2117 Fourth Street
Suite D
Berkeley, CA 94710

www.softskull.com
www.counterpointpress.com

Distributed by Publishers Group West

10 9 8 7 6 5 4 3 2 1

for the Art Stars

CONTENTS

A VERY BRIEF FOREWORD
by Jonathan Ames

I AM REVEREND Jen's literary agent, former lover, and ever-passionate admirer. In my humble opinion, she is one of the most remarkable human beings I've ever met. She is such a great artist that she *is* art. Her life is art. But this doesn't mean that she's just some mad eccentric. Well, she is a mad eccentric, but she is also a wildly productive artist: she makes gorgeous paintings; she writes essays, fiction, plays, television shows, puppet shows, and screenplays; she builds props and stage sets; she manages a troll museum; she publishes and edits *ASS Magazine*, which she founded; she performs as an actress, storyteller, comedienne, and author; she makes art books and *objets* that have been displayed in museums; she hosts a monthly open-mike performance show called "Reverend Jen's Anti-Slam," which has been going strong for twelve years; she directs her own plays, movies, and television shows. Essentially, she's a Picasso-like force of nature.

There's a performance art scene in New York City, which she has helped create, and the players in the scene are called "Art

Stars." They're the freakiest, most dysfunctional band of incredible lunatics, shining and exploding luminescently like human Northern Lights. No one has money, everyone barely gets by, the sexualities are as diverse as the insect world, and they all indefatigably produce the most outrageous performances, unparalleled in their creativity, humor, and beauty. They're a wild mix of comedians, singers, sketch artists, poets, and soapbox ranters. Rev. Jen came up with the term "Art Stars" in much the same way that Jack Kerouac coined the term "Beats," and in the scene, she's like the prime minister—she's Frank Sinatra, Mae West, Emma Peel, and Galadriel, all in one. She is beloved.

Now let's talk about her person. She's kind, humble, and forgiving. She drinks too much beer and she wears elf ears all the time. Her relationships with men (except for those who become her literary agent) are tormented and deranged. She barely gets by and has to work as a sexual surrogate to support herself, which means that she attends to men who go to a psychiatrist for a variety of sexual problems and masturbates them. Her dearest companion is her dog, a feisty and elegant chihuaha named Rev. Jen, Jr., who attends every show of the Art Stars, barking out her displeasure or her joy.

So that's something of a snapshot of my dear friend; it's not nearly voluminous enough, but I hope it gives you some idea of the extraordinary and unique author you are about to engage. I won't try to explain this book that you are holding; it can speak for itself and beautifully at that. I do think you will love it and come to love Rev. Jen, as well. I know I do.

Brooklyn, New York
February, 2009

1

NAKED LADIES
ARE COOL

AFTER A MOMENT'S deliberation, I typed:

> Adorable nude housecleaner will clean your pad spic-
> and-span for a reasonable fee. Available immediately.

I thought that "adorable" sounded less conceited than "hot" or "sexy." Plus, I figured men who were seeking nude housekeepers were probably looking more for June Cleaver than Jenna Jameson.

Moments later, a deluge of emails appeared in my inbox. Posting my ad on the coldest weekend of the year had been a stroke of genius. No one was planning to leave his or her apartment. The very idea that someone, anyone, was willing to go outside, let alone take off her clothes, was a phenomenon—a marketing blitz.

"Do you do bathtubs?" "What is your rate?" and "Can you send me a picture?" were the most common requests. Not knowing how much to charge, I looked to the other ads on craigslist, but all of the nude housecleaners simply wrote, "Email me for rates," with the exception of one nude house-cleaner who was offering his services for free.

"Ew!" exclaimed my coworker, Angie, who'd been hovering over my shoulder, reading the various ads. The going rate for clothed housekeepers was between $10 and $20 per hour.

"If they just took their clothes off, they could make a lot more money," I surmised. "Maybe they need a manager." $50 an hour seemed to be a fair price, if not a bit on the cheap side. But because my endeavor was really a science project, I didn't believe it was ethical to charge premium rates.

"What's the best way to clean a bathtub?" I asked Angie. (Not that I don't clean my bathtub; it's just that I clean my bathtub with no regard for whether or not I leave scratches.)

"Scrubbing Bubbles," she responded. "Definitely Scrubbing Bubbles."

"Really?" My mother had used Scrubbing Bubbles in the '70s, and I was sure bathtub-cleaning technology must have advanced since then. "What if I faint from the fumes? I don't want to end up naked and unconscious on the bathroom floor."

"Maybe you should wear one of those paper masks," she suggested.

"That's not really erotic, is it?" I was going to look silly enough bent over in unflattering positions, my loose flesh flapping about. I didn't need to compound the ridiculousness with a mask.

After work, I went by the drugstore to peruse the cleaning-supply section. Much to my surprise, I noticed that Scrubbing Bubbles had multiplied into an entire line of products, including toilet brushes, Fizz-Its toilet tablets, and mildew-stain removers. The new products featured angry-looking bubble mascots with arched eyebrows and aggressive expressions. I wondered if the new, evil-looking bubbles were a reflection of American politicians in the new millennium—at war with an unseen enemy, going about their business blindly, only to be washed down the drain eventually. I was overcome with sadness. Then I realized that the old-school Scrubbing Bubbles canister still featured the happy-looking, bristle-mustachioed bubbles of yore. This cheered me.

On my way home from the drugstore, I stopped in at the local video store, hoping to pick up a copy of *Maid in Manhattan* for inspiration. Maybe my first client would be a Ralph Fiennes look-alike who would whisk me out of destitution and into a life of leisure and couture. Predictably, I could not locate said J. Lo vehicle—this being a downtown hipster video store—and I was too embarrassed to ask the surly cashier if they carried it. Instead I rented *Murderous Maids*, a French film about two incestuous sisters who are also maids and kill their employers. Probably a little more realistic.

At home I slipped into my footie pajamas and popped open my laptop, whereupon I began emailing current photos of myself to potential employers. I made an appointment with Tony, who wanted to see me the next day at the unreasonable hour of 9:30 AM. We agreed on a minimum of two hours of cleaning.

Another potential client named Ryan—who had yet to see my photo—sent me his cell phone number and requested I call immediately. I dialed the number.

Ryan insisted he needed his apartment cleaned that night, no later than 10 PM. It was now eight-thirty. I hesitated. For starters, I hadn't washed my hair in two days and had begun to resemble a lost member of the Manson family. Not to mention the five o'clock shadow that had begun to form around my pudenda. I imagined that greeting a client with a stubbly vag was a nude-housecleaning faux pas. How I would get cleaned up and get uptown in under two hours was beyond me, but I agreed to it.

"I just have two main concerns," Ryan said before giving me his address. "The first is that while you claim you're 'adorable,' I worry that you'll show up and look like Jabba the Hutt."

I assured him that I was not a legless, tapered slug covered in slime, but rather more like Princess Leia, and could even wear my long, raven hair in dual buns if he so desired. This cinched the deal. Within every man who was breathing during the early '80s, there lies dormant a terrible fear of Jabba the Hutt and an overwhelming fixation with Princess Leia. (Specifically when she is bound in chains by the gruesome Jabba; it's the greatest BDSM scene in cinematic history.)

"I do have small breasts, so if you want a nude house-cleaner with huge breasts, that's not me. Plus, I have a crazy scar on my stomach." I figured it was best to get these two things out of the way immediately.

"That's okay, but my other concern," he added, "is that because you are going to be naked, you won't do a good job cleaning my apartment."

"You have nothing to worry about," I assured him. Secretly, I thought, *Oh shit, he really wants me to clean.* Cleaning, unlike getting naked, is an actual skill I wasn't sure I'd mastered. I jotted down Ryan's address, leapt off the phone, and quickly Googled "how to clean wooden floors." What if I ruined his fancy Upper East Side apartment?

I gussied up in record time and ran to the train. My

bladder began to swell with urgency; I had traveled outside my "pee radius." My mind raced with concerns. Would his apartment be well heated? Would he be a sociopath? Would he get a boner? Would he *not* get a boner? Would he want me to polish his family jewels? Would I get turned on?

Exiting the train, I turned the corner onto Madison Avenue and strolled past a group of mink-clad women. My tattered faux-fur coat and pink-streaked hair made me feel conspicuous. *I hope the doorman realizes I'm not a prostitute,* I thought.

But what if I *were* a prostitute? It's nothing to be ashamed of. At least prostitutes get to lie down on the job. Here, I'd be naked and scrubbing toilets. Prostitutes would laugh at me. As sex work goes, naked housecleaning is as low as it gets on the food chain. Except for the guy who used to pay to lick cum off peepshow stalls in the Times Square of yesteryear. That guy is just below me on the sex-work ladder.

When Ryan answered the door, I was delighted to see that he was a preppy redhead. Even though I tend to date men who are more like the Fonz, I am most attracted to Richie Cunningham types—wholesome redheads. (I know that Ralph Malph was also a redhead, but I preferred Richie's dry sense of humor to Ralph's reliance on sight gags.) Sadly, the Richie Cunninghams of the world want nothing to do with me.

"Is it warm enough for you?" Ryan asked shyly, as I ran to his bathroom to relieve myself. "There are a lot of elderly people in this building, so I don't even need to turn my heat on."

"Do you think they'd want their apartments cleaned?" I asked.

"Probably not," he replied.

As I ambled out of his bathroom, I began to remove my clothing in a manner that was matter-of-fact and probably unerotic, perhaps because I was now wearing giant yellow dishwashing gloves. Sort of a shame, since my hands are my best feature. I'd planned to bring a pair of silver stilettos along but had forgotten them in the mad rush uptown.

As for Ryan's apartment, it didn't look dirty. In fact, it seemed cleaner than my own.

"Do you like wine?" he asked.

I know I shouldn't have accepted a glass of wine from a stranger with whom I was now naked in a strange apartment far from my home, but the answer slipped out before logic could catch up with my mouth. "Yes, I like wine very much," I answered, suddenly feeling like a gullible protagonist in an ABC *After School Special*.

"Great, I have some white wine in the fridge. Only problem is there are no clean glasses to drink it out of."

In the history of the world, I don't think two glasses have ever been cleaned as quickly as they were at that moment. Within seconds, we were sipping wine from two sparkling, streak-free goblets.

"Cheers!" Ryan pronounced as we clinked glasses.

"Back to work," I said, pouring dishwashing liquid onto the plates in his sink.

"Whoa!" he exclaimed. "That dishwashing liquid is very thick. It leaves film on the plates if you use too much."

Was Ryan here to bask in the glow of my nakedness or to backseat-drive my every move? Would he soon slip on a white glove and follow me around like Leona Helmsley checking for dust marks at the Park Lane Hotel? The distasteful Joy brand dishwashing liquid featured a sunglasses-sporting lemon on the label. "I don't like the looks of that guy," I said, noting the lemon's malicious grin. Apparently an evil-mascot trend is afoot in the world of cleaning products.

"I got it at the ninety-nine-cent store," Ryan admitted.

"You should never buy your cleaning supplies at the ninety-nine-cent store. I've made that mistake. Things always end up sticky or smelly." I diluted the Joy with water and continued scrubbing. The silence grew.

"Why did you hire a naked cleaning lady as opposed to a regular cleaning lady?" I finally inquired.

"I guess it's just cool to have a naked lady around."

"Naked ladies are cool," I agreed. Truer words were never spoken.

"Plus," he noted, "I like the way your breasts jiggle when you scrub the dishes."

"My breasts don't really jiggle," I said, calmly scouring a serving plate. "I've been wearing a training bra since I was thirteen."

"They jiggle enough for me."

I looked down. Sure enough, each swipe of the Brillo pad facilitated a chain reaction.

"Tell me about your scar," Ryan suggested.

"A lot of people think it's a C-section scar, but it's actually from a ruptured appendix. The doctors misdiagnosed my stomach pains as gas, and a few hours later I was chewing Pepcid ACs at home when it burst. Soon thereafter, gangrenated appendix matter poisoned my blood. I almost died."

If Ryan had a boner, it must have wilted as I described the oozing, bloody hole on my stomach that I was forced to pack daily with Bacitracin-covered gauze. When I looked up from my monologue, his face was sheet white. He looked like he was going to be ill.

"If you squint, my scar actually looks like a second ass," I offered.

"Yeah, except for the belly button," he concurred, squinting.

I handed him the last of the dishes, which he dutifully dried. "What's next?"

After I scoured the microwave and countertop, Ryan refilled my wineglass and checked his watch. When you're paying fifty bucks an hour, it's important to prioritize. "Well, we don't have time for laundry," he deduced. I heaved a massive sigh of relief. When it comes to cleaning, laundry is my Achilles' heel. I guessed Ryan wouldn't be too pleased about wearing a toddler-sized shirt to work on Monday.

"Your floors look very shiny and clean," I noted, attempting to save myself from cleaning them.

"Yeah, they're pretty clean. I guess we'll move on to the bathroom."

In the bathroom, I pulled out my weaponry—the Scrubbing Bubbles I'd become so emotionally involved with—and sprayed a heavy layer onto the bathtub's surface.

"What does it do now?" he asked.

"It does the work for us," I said. "Which means I can move on to the sink."

As I scoured the sink, Ryan and I chatted like old friends. Maybe it was because we were the same age, or maybe it was because we bonded over the varying levels of high-SPF sunscreen I found in his cabinet, but I felt comfortable around him.

"This SPF 30 looks a little old. You might wanna throw it out," I said.

"I didn't realize I would get a running commentary on the products in my bathroom."

"What's this? Hydrating seaweed and mineral-water spray? Do you actually use this?"

"No, and I have no idea where it came from. Do you want it?"

"Sure!"

Once we'd fully exhausted the topic of his cabinet contents, the conversation turned to love woes, ambitions, and desires. We veered from mindless chatter into deep conversation. Like Alice consoling Jan over an unrequited love on *The Brady Bunch*, I consoled Ryan over his hankering for his ex-girlfriend, and he listened as I described my exasperatingly unpredictable love life. "Do you ever want to get married?" I asked.

"Yeah, you?"

"Yeah, but only so I can wear a pink mini-dress and matching veil to my wedding."

What life choices had we made, we pondered, that had brought us to this strange point in our lives? We were both thirty-two, single, and living in opposite tax brackets and neighborhoods, yet our lives had intersected in a city of millions.

I didn't tell him I was really on assignment. Nude housecleaning was the first of many experiments I'd be performing for Nerve.com's "I Did It for Science," a monthly column for which I would embark on various sexual misadventures. This truth, I thought, would make Ryan go flaccid.

So I told him I'd become a nude housecleaner in order to pay my overdue medical bills—not entirely untrue. I owed the hospital approximately $50,000 and "The Man" had recently seized my bank account.

Ryan listened intently and maybe the wine or the cleaning fumes impaired my judgment, or maybe I thought it would make the story more sordid, but I desperately wanted to kiss him at that moment, even though he claimed he was holding out for that special someone—an actual girlfriend or, in the best possible scenario, his ex-girlfriend, whom he still loved. This just made me crazier, as it fulfilled every Richie Cunningham fantasy I'd harbored since well before puberty. And the worst part was that Ryan seemed to think of me as his naked friend, platonically hanging out with him in the bathroom.

I triumphantly ran my Scotch-Brite pad over the tub. "I can see myself," I marveled. Indeed, his bathtub gleamed like Oz in the distance, but as I stood up, the resulting head-rush almost knocked me off my feet. Maybe the paper-mask idea hadn't been such a bad one.

Ryan glanced at his watch. I figured that he didn't want to spend a thousand dollars for me to chitchat his ear off all night while simultaneously emptying his wine rack. As we left the bathroom, I walked over to his bed and laid down. "I think I'm inebriated," I said bluntly.

Either Ryan was the most gentlemanly human alive—or he just thought I was a pathetic nude-housecleaning whore—but nothing actually happened, even though I suggested we do some necking. "Don't you want to make out with me?" I asked from the edge of his bed, still wearing the giant yellow gloves.

"I think it's really cool that my nude housecleaner is coming on to me, but I can't. You can sleep over if you need to," he offered.

"I have to get home to my Chihuahua. We've never spent a night apart," I explained, searching for the contents of my wardrobe and tossing my bra into my purse.

"In that case, I insist you take a cab. I'll pay for it."

He escorted me out the door and put me in a cab. As the trees of Central Park East disappeared behind me, I felt a little sad about the whole experience. Maybe it was the way Alice felt after consoling Jan, when she realized she really wasn't part of the Brady Bunch. She could serve them dinner but could never eat with them, because she was a servant. And that's exactly what I had been, no matter how much I enjoyed it.

The following day, my "nature sounds" alarm clock announced the ungodly hour of 8 AM with a cock's crow. In a haze, I stumbled to the shower. Suddenly nude house-cleaning didn't look so fun now that it was morning and I was hungover. However, upon opening my purse to retrieve my lipstick, I realized I had two fresh fifty-dollar bills. This made my scientific endeavor seem a lot more worthwhile.

Today, my nude housecleaning would be like a mafia hit. I would get in and out as quickly as possible—no wine, no deep conversation, no yukkin' it up. When I arrived at my destination, I was shocked to discover that my client lived in the very hotel where I'd had my first same-sex experience. (Long story: I slept next to a bald lesbian named Pam and we touched each other's "parts.") Because the security guard seemed to be dozing off—much like me—I made my way to the third floor, where Tony greeted me at his door.

While Tony wasn't physically offensive, he was definitely not my type. I like my men breakable and spindly, with skin that looks like it's spent several years fading in a cave. Tony was tan and muscular. He walked with the pigeon-toed gait of someone who went to the gym twice a day. Sure enough, I spied muscle-building protein formula on top of his fridge and was immediately turned off.

This, coupled with the fact that my libido doesn't work until after 5 PM, meant that I was in for a mundane two hours. *I've got to clean as quickly as possible and then get the hell home to my bed*, I thought, stripping my clothes off and laying them on a chair.

Apparently my arrival had interrupted Tony's cartoon watching, as he immediately reclined on his chair and recommenced watching *Pokémon*.

"I usually have a clothed cleaning girl do this," he explained. "But I saw your ad and thought this might be fun for a change." He instructed me to start with his bathroom, mainly the bathtub. Apparently, all men passionately detest bathtub cleaning. (Since my tryst with nude housecleaning, I have conferred with other males on this subject, and they have professed that this is 100 percent true.)

I repeated the various steps I had performed only a few hours earlier at Ryan's, letting those crazy bubbles initiate their war on germs while I sponged little black hairs away. Pikachu giggled like a schoolgirl in the distance as I sprayed Windex onto the mirror, revealing a reflection of myself wherein I looked old and tragic.

There truly isn't much to report from this session, save the various steps I followed to sterilize Tony's apartment. At one point, I cleaned Tony's bedroom mirror with a glass cleaner whose label declared it was for the bathroom, whereupon he tried to stop me. I had to explain that just because a cleaning product declared it was for the bathroom, that didn't mean you couldn't use it in the bedroom, and vice versa. As long as you don't mix bleach and ammonia, it should be smooth sailing.

Vacuuming followed bathroom sterilization, which was followed by dusting. I'm sorry if I've given the collective readership of this story a softie, but I was bored out of my mind, too. After almost an hour, I announced that I was finished and reached for my panties. "Hmm, we've still got fifteen minutes," Tony declared, checking his watch. "You don't do anything besides cleaning, do you?"

I wasn't sure if this question meant, "Do you do anything sexual besides cleaning?" or "Do you do other things in general besides cleaning?" I was about to say, "Well, I like to walk my dog, paint, and eat a lot of Mexican food" when I noticed the lascivious expression on Tony's face.

I think he wanted a blowjob. But I will never know, because he didn't ask, and I certainly wasn't going to suggest it. When requesting sexual favors from your nude housecleaner—or from anyone at all—it's important to be as specific as possible. "How about a back massage?" I proposed.

Removing my yellow gloves, I rubbed my hands together and worked my fingers down into his back. "You do that really well," he sighed, a smile crossing his lips. Maybe he wouldn't notice the shitty job I did cleaning his floor.

After a fifteen-minute rubdown, Tony stood up and handed me a fifty-dollar bill with a totally dissatisfied look. "You said no funny business," he smiled, shrugging.

I was happy to get dressed and flee from his apartment. After only two sessions, nude housecleaning had lost its novelty. Whether you're naked, clothed, or half-dressed, cleaning is actual work. The two main bonuses to cleaning naked: you won't soil your clothes, and you'll make $30 more per hour than a regular maid.

As I walked from Tony's to the subway, the cold air froze my face and my teeth actually chattered. It was too cold to be naked anywhere, indoors or out. Ducking into Hot &

Crusty for a cup of hot tea, I had the distinct feeling that I never wanted to get naked or clean another apartment again. For the next week, I thought, the only sponge I want to see wears square pants and works at the Krusty Krab.

At home, I opened my laptop and deleted a slew of other nude housecleaning requests. Slipping back into my footie pajamas, I commenced writing my article, wondering just what in the hell I had gotten myself into.

2   ART FAG

DESPITE THE FACT that *Sex and the City* convinced viewers that being a sex columnist in New York City is cool, it wasn't a job I went looking for. Since coming to New York City in 1990, I'd take basically any job I could get. And sex columnist happened to be one of them. If anything, it was remarkably similar to the other humiliating jobs I'd worked. These include, but aren't limited to: Christmas elf at Bloomingdale's, leprechaun at an Irish pub, security guard at the Metropolitan Museum of Art, children's TV show extra, body painter, and giant frog at the Central Park Zoo (which entailed walking around in a frog costume that smelled like vomit while children beat and made fun of me). By the time I landed the gig at Nerve, I'd also acquired a relatively sane part-time job at a bookstore: a real step up, considering it didn't involve a silly costume.

It's not surprising that I became such an outstanding underachiever, given the fact that my childhood heroes were all underachieving TV characters. Like most kids who grew up in the '70s, I didn't want to be president, but I did want to be the Fonz—a grownup whose "office" was the bathroom at Arnold's Drive-In. Mr. Kotter, Laverne, Shirley, Jack Tripper, Lenny, and Squiggy may not have been rich, but their lives weren't boring, and that, I determined, trumped success.

Avoiding boredom became my singular goal in life. Upon seeing Andy Warhol do a cameo on *The Love Boat*, I realized the best way to achieve this goal was to become an artist. So I spent most of my time painting and drawing, creative activities viewed with suspicion in suburban Maryland. Further disconcerted by my fondness for wearing flamboyant clothes, most people assumed I was either on drugs or a Satanist.

When I was sixteen, the cool kids in my high school painted the phrase "You are a art fag" on the street in front of my family's house. I knew it was the cool kids because of the grammatical error. It should have been *an* art fag. The words were so big you could have spotted them from an airplane. Because the street was state property, uniformed men came to our house and graveled over it. To the uniformed men pouring gravel, it was just another day combating vandalism in a town where vandalism is one of the few creative activities anyone engages in. To me, it was a historic event that propelled me to get the hell out of Maryland at any cost.

The following year I escaped to New York City, where I enrolled in the School of Visual Arts, with hopes of becoming an art star. (An art star is what happens when an "art fag" escapes a hostile environment and blossoms.) I arrived in 1990, too late for the salons of Greenwich Village, the Beats, Studio 54, or punk rock. New York was a city on the verge of becoming less cool than me.

Because the School of Visual Arts didn't have student housing, I took a room at the Parkside Evangeline, a Salvation Army residence for women. I didn't know anyone in New York. To make matters worse, the Parkside was an all-female residence. It was like *Bosom Buddies*, only there was no Tom Hanks or other guy to keep me company. Whatever feminist coined the phrase "a woman without a man is like a fish without a bicycle" never visited the Parkside. I had been told that the Parkside was a residence for young women but found many of the residents there to be elderly women who had lived there *since* they were young women, and who had since that time developed romantic liaisons with other formerly young, now elderly residents. This produced a constant stream of softcore elderly porn in the cafeteria, lobby, and elevators.

Eventually I made one friend there my age, a fellow SVA student named Juliette. Each night we met in the cafeteria where we observed the freaks who populated the Parkside—not the tattooed, pierced freaks one might expect to find in New York, but freaks like the woman who attended dinner every night with her entire head, hair included, covered in Vaseline. She also had a wacky habit of dumping buckets of ice-cold water out her window onto unsuspecting pedestrians. Many residents looked like the zombies in Michael Jackson's "Thriller" video. We terrified each other by contriving ghost stories about our neighbors. Juliette even claimed to have seen one of them fly off the roof and turn into a bat.

Juliette and I were inseparable until she fell for a dude and I was, once again, totally alone. I'd come all the way to New York City only to live in an insane asylum with elderly lesbians and have my one friend abandon me for a penis.

I was so lonely that I called my parents and told them I wanted to come home at the end of the year.

But before that could happen, I met a group of film students who took me under their wing and introduced me to a new best friend: LSD. I fell so in love with it that I spent the next four months eating as much of it as I could obtain. Since it only cost about a dollar a hit, that equaled a lot. And what I couldn't pay for I obtained by writing term papers for wealthy students who were too stoned to focus on Euripides. (Pretty much everyone at SVA.) They paid me in LSD, mescaline, or hash.

One night, a film student named Karen invited Juliette and me to a party at a building where a number of SVA students lived. I forget what I drank that night, but by the time I got there, I was drunk. The dude who opened the door to let us in had long, flowing dirty-blond hair and a handlebar mustache. Everyone called him Dog, which I learned was short for his longer nickname: Dog P.

I went into Dog P.'s bedroom and smoked a joint with him. We closed the door, took off our clothes, and made love. We kissed on the lips like we'd been separated for centuries and were finally reunited. We lay in bed, holding each other until the pot mixed with the booze made me suddenly queasy and I leaned over and vomited in a cup next to his bed. He moved the violated cup away from the bed and put his arms around me. And as he did, I felt another visceral reaction similar to nausea: I was in love.

And I never wanted to leave New York City again.

Dog and I spent hours in bed, talking and making love. Sometimes he took his fingers and marched them tenderly across my belly, enacting scenes from *The Dark Crystal.*

He pretended his hands were Landstriders carrying the Gelflings across my skin to safety. We spoke in made-up elfin languages to each other, sometimes singing lightly in our invented tongue into each other's ears.

One Valentine's Day, he tied a dozen trolls to rose stems and gave me a bouquet of trolls.

Dog's pride in his own resplendent uncoolness inspired me to combat the pseudo-nonconformity of my classmates who all rebelled in exactly the same way: black clothing, piercings, and tattoos. Soon I began wearing prosthetic elf ears to school. No one else wore elf ears. I don't remember the exact reason why I started wearing them or where I bought them. The only solid thing I can remember from art school is that a forty of King Cobra malt liquor cost $1.63.

So for whatever reason, elf ears became a permanent part of my wardrobe.

3

COLLECTIVE UNCONSCIOUS

IN THE EARLY '90s every art student in the world wanted to be either Matthew Barney or Basquiat. The kids who wanted to be Matthew Barney spent a lot of money on their art and the kids who wanted to be Basquiat spent a lot of money on heroin. I had never done heroin and planned on never doing heroin. I was not cool enough to be either Barney or Basquiat.

I signed up for a performance art class taught by art-world luminary Mike Smith, which only about five other people signed up for. People did outrageous things and Mike Smith encouraged it. One pupil, Jason Pilarski, who lived with Beat legend Herbert Huncke, went to the bathroom, peed on his poem, and then read the pee-soaked poem to the class. Jason once did a sculpture that he attached to the couch in the SVA sculpture building. It was a mess of wires, pipes, and metal and it was leaking liquid onto the floor. As his fellow students railed on him during a critique he calmly said, "I made the sculpture to go with the painting." He pointed to the furthest corner of the ceiling and there, barely visible, was a small nondescript painting. "Performance art," Mike Smith explained, "is about becoming a giant asshole." This concept thrilled me because most contemporary art was austere, slick, and superficial. I went to galleries every week and they were filled with minimal pieces that were all about artists pretending like they didn't have assholes.

Making pictures no longer held much interest for me. I wanted to move off the canvas, to make living art, to be living art, and in the end, make things that reflected this. I wanted to be a performance artist, which is really the least lucrative thing a human being can decide to do. Like the elf ears, it seemed like a good idea at the time.

Juliette was also getting into performance art. One day we decided to start a band. The fact that neither of us could sing or play an instrument did not deter us. Together we formed Pop Rox, a band so terrible that we put a lock on the door wherever we were performing and literally locked our audience in to ensure they wouldn't walk out. We played "gigs" in the classrooms at SVA or by crashing parties where people screamed at us to shut up.

Feeling that we were now experts in uncoolness, we penned a short book: the bible of the uncool. Then we sent a dollar each to the Universal Life Church, a church that will ordain anyone. Within a week, I received my certificate of ordination in the mail. I was now Reverend Jen Miller, a legal Reverend.

After graduation Juliette and I both got crap retail jobs where, each day, our dreams of becoming art stars died just a little more. Pop Rox crumbled under the pressure and broke up. Juliette moved upstate and had a baby. I, on the other hand, was determined to keep performing.

Collective Unconscious was a rundown art-hole theater that had formerly been a brothel fronting as a tailor shop, but it's where I ended up after Pop Rox broke up. My friend Monica recommended I attend the open mike there, which was run by a performance artist named Faceboy. I was wary, expecting to wander into a room filled with bongo-playing, finger-snapping poets who, in an attempt to appear cool, were regressing to a much cooler era by emulating the poetry-reading style of Kerouac and Ginsberg. I wanted to progress even if it meant facing the fact that my own era is totally lame.

But a few acts into the show all I could think was, *so this is where art went.*

I became a regular at Faceboy's. Before his open mike, I'd felt like de Sade writing in prison—hopeless. But now people were seeing my work. I was asked to perform in shows and at art galleries around the city. A theater producer named Tom Tenney produced my first plays, *Halitonia* and *Lord of the Cockrings*, and Faceboy helped me start my own weekly open mike, Reverend Jen's Anti-Slam. Unlike the then-popular poetry slams where writers competed, the Anti-Slam promised every performer a perfect score of ten.

My show attracted the outcasts among outcasts. You will never hear me utter the phrase, "I have seen it all," because just when I think I've seen it all, I see a man gallop onto the stage in a Speedo and proceed to explain Hegel while simultaneously pouring baking soda and vinegar into his Speedo, causing a children's science fair–like volcanic explosion to occur within his swimsuit, which will then begin to seep out of the tiny holes in the Speedo's fabric and explode on the stage, causing the first row of audience members to run in terror.

No, I have not seen everything, but I have seen a woman paint a penis onto canvas with her menstrual blood, a man paint his penis purple, a man light a match in his pee-hole, a man pull a fish out of his pants, an audience member accidentally drink a performer's pee, performers purposefully drink each other's pee, and performers drink douche. I have witnessed eggs, onions, and olives pulled from orifices. I have also seen brilliant comedy, dance, onstage weddings, music, and poetry. I have been driven to nausea and inspired.

I began to refer to every performer who got up onstage as an "art star," and the scene centering around the open mikes soon became known as "the art star scene." Eventually I started a zine, *Art Star Scene Magazine*, or *ASS*. It featured a different art star's ass on the cover of each issue.

The art star scene provided me with an artistic community I hadn't had in art school, a legion of like-minded lunatics who wanted to collaborate. I was living in Brooklyn but eventually moved to the neighborhood that was at the center of the art star scene: Manhattan's Lower East Side.

In the early '90s the Lower East Side was still a junkie's paradise paved with overflowing garbage and dilapidated buildings, so the rent was cheap.

My new roommate seemed like a nice girl until the day she came home with a stick of dynamite tattooed on her forearm and announced she was an anarchist. A few days later she tried to kill me by banging my head into the concrete wall of our kitchen. While this incident probably left me with permanent brain damage, it also left me with the lease to a rent-stabilized apartment in Manhattan.

In the flurry of activity, Dog and I split up. Actually I did the breaking up, and I'm not sure why, considering I still loved him. Maybe I broke up with him because I thought my life should be more adventurous. Or it could have been because he had California and success on his horizon and I had the Lower East Side and instability on mine.

He was the only boyfriend I'd ever had and I had no idea what assholes other men were. Plus, I thought if it were meant to be, it would be. Now I realize this is an idiotic concept.

A brilliant twenty-three-year-old straight man with a job in New York is rare, and no one ever told me about cleanup women. A cleanup woman (or man) is the lover who comes along after the original lover has either broken up with or mistreated their lover. After I broke up with Dog, the cleanup woman came along and the two eventually married.

When my appendix ruptured a few years later, I realized something about love. Love is like the human appendix. You take it for granted while it's there, but when it's suddenly gone you're forced to endure horrible pain that can only be alleviated through drugs.

4 THE MIDWAY MOTEL

AFTER DOG AND I split, I spent most of my time with Faceboy. When I first met him, I thought he was the coolest person on the Lower East Side. Then he invited me to a cast
party following a play he'd directed. Only one other person
showed up at his party. That's when I realized we would be
best friends.

I also spent a lot of time with Tom Tenney, the scene's
"producer"; Bruce, the scene's only audience member (who
didn't perform, himself); and a woman named Kat, who
looked like a vixen out of a Russ Meyer movie and who doc-
umented much of the scene's insanity with her video camera.
We spent a lot of time drinking Budweiser, which is sold
in a vast array of sizes at Lower East Side bodegas. There
are eight-ounce, ten-ounce, twelve-ounce, sixteen-ounce,
twenty-four-ounce, thirty-two-ounce and forty-ounce varieties, just to name a few.

Under the influence of these ounces, I made many unwise
choices in love. For a year I cozied up to a celibate man who

wouldn't fuck me and was incarcerated in Rikers Island for most of our relationship. Then I moved on to a married man who dumped me for a woman who wasn't even his wife. Giving up on men, I dated a stunning bisexual woman who turned out to be insane, whereupon I gained the wisdom that comes from being bisexual and recognizing that men and women are equally fucked up.

It didn't take me long to realize one thing: whoever said things can only get better never dated in New York.

Despite romantic setbacks, I never quit producing shit-loads of art. At one point, I even turned the front room of my apartment into a Troll Museum where I displayed my collection of 400 troll dolls alongside paintings I'd done of them. Everyone wanted to visit the Troll Museum. One day I got an email from an underground filmmaker named Nick Zedd, requesting a visit. I'd met him briefly on the set of a Troma movie I was in. The first time I saw him he was wearing a *Bride of Frankenstein* wig and lab coat, examining a pregnant Toxic Avenger who was about to give birth to a midget in a Toxic Avenger mask. I thought Nick was dreamy—wide blue eyes, high cheekbones and full lips. He looked vampiric, like his skin hadn't seen sunlight in twenty years.

When he came to the Troll Museum, I invited him to a Valentine's Day party a few nights later. At the party he asked me to be his Valentine, took me home, and fucked me like only a crazy person can. I hadn't dated anyone in three years and I fell for him, mostly because he was the strangest person I'd ever met.

Our relationship was doomed from day one. He lived with Isabelle, his ex-girlfriend. They had lived together for eleven years in an apartment that cost roughly $300. Real estate in New York City will make people who hate each other stay together.

Isabelle was beautiful, French, and insane. When she found out Nick and I were dating, she took to torturing me. She played Serge Gainsbourg records into my answering machine at 3 AM and left messages calling me "ugly American trash."

Isabelle wasn't my only opposition. Nick had ex-girlfriends all over the city. They were everywhere, badass buxom punk girls who wanted me dead.

One night Nick and I were sitting in a bar when a fat woman in tight leopard-print pants, who was missing a front tooth, strolled in and screamed, "Nick, what are you doing here with this woman? You told me last week you would love me forever!"

Episodes like this became common.

Nick and I began making movies together, which put an even greater strain on our relationship. Many shoots ended with props being hurled and obscenities exchanged. Among the cinematic gems we turned out were *Elf Panties: The Movie* and *Lord of the Cockrings*, the film version of my take on Tolkien. Before the premiere of *Lord of the Cockrings*, Nick stole a giant cardboard cutout of the hobbits from New Line's *Lord of the Rings* movie out of a movie theater's lobby and gave it to me as a present.

Sometimes he shoplifted flowers and stuffed them under my coat.

But these loving gestures hardly made up for the way he treated me. If we were watching TV, he would point to a voluptuous actress and say, "That looks like Isabelle." Then he'd point to Granny from the *Beverly Hillbillies* and say,

"That looks like you." My self-esteem grew so low, I didn't think anyone else would want me.

Looking back, I wonder why I stayed, and why women in general stay with assholes. My conclusion is that women stay with assholes because assholes don't leave. Once an asshole has figured out he can jizz in your hair, empty your fridge, and run up your phone bill, he's not going anywhere. And that's vaguely comforting.

Nice guys leave to "find themselves," but assholes never look for themselves.

When I complained about Nick to Tom, he said, "Well *you* manifested him."

"What are you talking about?"

"When I asked you what you wanted in a boyfriend, you said 'someone weird with a big dick.'"

"But I wanted someone nice too."

"Well, you have be specific when you ask the universe for something."

I went home and made a list of what I wanted in a man. It was four words long: *Nice, Tender, Honest, Beautiful.*

I put the list under my pillow and went to sleep.

I was pretty sure Nick was screwing other women, though he denied it. Then one morning I peeked in his journal. It's a breach of trust to do this, but it's also a breach of trust to fuck everything east of the Bowery behind your loving, monogamous elf girlfriend's back. On every page he described fucking someone other than me—Isabelle, the girl in leopard-print pants, and an assortment of others with low self-esteem.

I put the journal down and commenced having a mild breakdown. Tom and Bruce came to get me. They took me and my newly adopted Chihuahua, JJ (short for Reverend Jen Junior), on a road trip to Pennsylvania to see the Charlie Daniels Band, which I love, perform at the Pat Garrett Roadhouse Saloon.

We rented a room at the Midway Motel along Route 78. The Midway had clearly been built in the '50s and had not been renovated or cleaned since. Many of the windows were boarded up. It was like the set of *Psycho*. Our room contained a bloody sheet draped over a broken air conditioner.

Before the show we drank some beer and each took a tiny dose of magic mushrooms. We only wanted to get a tiny buzz from the shrooms, but when you're dealing with fungi you can never be quite sure how hard they'll hit.

Still sober and in touch with reality, Tom, Bruce, and I left for the Pat Garrett Saloon, just up the road. Almost immediately upon entering the amphitheater, which was filled with good ol' boys, the shrooms kicked in harder than anything I have ever taken or experienced in my life. I looked at Tom and Bruce. They were thinking the same thing: "HOLY SHIT!"

We attempted to put a blanket down among the crowd, but we were like infants who were amazed and terrified. In my waking state I am frightened of Republicans, and now I was surrounded by them TRIPPING. We agreed that we had to get away from people right away, so we went to the farthest corner of a field where people had parked their cars. We had just paid $20 to sit as far away from the concert as possible.

We lost our minds. I talked to blades of grass, had a past-life regression in which I saw myself as an old Native American woman, cried my eyes out, thought Charlie Daniels was God, and felt love pour in and out of me. I lay back with my head on the grass and touched the earth with my hands. I was connected to the earth and the sky. We shared the same energy. I could see and feel oneness.

When the shrooms wore off, Bruce, Tom, and I spent the next two days partying with our neighbors, year-round Midway residents. There were Frank, Rob, Danny, and a blonde girl sitting on top of a car. All of them were on parole. At some point I went into the room to get more beer, and Tom came bolting in seconds later.

"You gotta see this, Rev.! They are *pissing* on one of their neighbors!" he exclaimed.

I followed Tom and Bruce to a room at the end of the row, where an open door revealed "Matt," who lay upon his disheveled bed covered in pee. Apparently one of the local forms of entertainment was pissing on Matt, who had a habit of drinking himself into a state where he passed out with his door open.

"Son of a bitch deserves it! We're gonna piss on him tomorrow night, too. Stupid fuck," Rob said. I wondered if they derived sexual pleasure from this sadistic act, but it seemed far more mundane for them, like watching a baseball game or playing ping-pong. From that moment on, we joked about peeing on Matt as if a toilet weren't even an alternative.

"Have you seen Matt?" I asked Tom. "I have to pee."

Moments later, Matt emerged from his room, a fresh-faced blond in jeans and no shirt with a well-sculpted yet skinny physique. Immediately, the Midway regulars began poking fun at him. Rob even began to push him, threatening to kick his ass for no reason other than that he happened to be Matt.

"We are in the middle of a *Cops* episode," Tom said.

My troubles in New York seemed very small compared to those of Matt, who served as a wee-wee pad for his companions every night. We had just met true nihilists. The following day, as we sobered up and left the Midway, Bruce turned to me and said, "I don't know why anyone still goes to the Hamptons."

5

GREAT SEXPECTATIONS

WHEN I RETURNED Nick asked me to marry him. I said no. Yet I was so full of love from my recent hallucinatory experience that I said we could still be lovers. I was done with boyfriends. I wanted lovers and lots of them. I wanted adventure, to live like a pirate and answer to no one. This was something I'd decided while talking to a blade of grass in Pat Garrett's parking lot. I was sure that through one blade of grass the entire Universe could hear me.

And it had an answer.

I ran into Ada Calhoun, who'd interviewed me for *New York*. She was now an editor for Nerve.com, the website famous for getting people laid through online personals. She suggested I pitch some stories to them.

Nerve hired me to review books, including a dozen books on how to be a better lover. One book on fellatio had me lifting an empty half-gallon container tied to a string, with my tongue.

I started pitching essays based on my experiences. I sent

Ada one about a road trip I took to the X-Day celebration of the Church of the Subgenius with my friend Tommy Bigfinger. There we dropped acid and waited for aliens to abduct us while cavorting with naked hippies.

She read it, called me, and said, "We've got a job you'd be perfect for."

I went by Nerve's office, where Ada and Nerve's editor in chief, Michael Martin, told me they were looking for a woman to write a column called "I Did It for Science." I would embark on sexual adventures and report on them as though I'd just conducted a scientific experiment. Each story would have a hypothesis, results, and conclusion.

Previously, a charming Englishman named Grant Stoddard had written the column. Since I'd never trolled the internet for dates, I hadn't read anything on Nerve. Ada suggested I read Grant's work.

I went home and read his essays. They were hilarious and it appeared he'd gotten a lot of ass writing them.

I told Ada to sign me up.

6

FELLATIO SCHOOL

THE BIGGEST CHALLENGE of writing the gender-reassigned "I Did it For Science" was finding experiments Grant hadn't tried. It seemed he'd done everything from boning a sex doll to casting his own member using a "make your own dildo" kit and then literally fucking himself with it. After my stint with nude housecleaning, it appeared there was nothing left for me to do, save prostituting myself on the West Side Highway or letting someone pee on me.

Ada tried to get a high-end dildo store to give me $300 vibrators to "try out," but they refused.

Luckily, there was fellatio—something Grant, a straight man, hadn't done. When Ada sent me an Evite for a class on how to give better blowjobs, I knew it was time to strap on my thinking cap, dust off the Trapper Keeper, and bust out the kneepads. In comparison to my fine arts education, a class in fellatio sounded useful. Sucking dick is a skill that can be employed time and time again to great effect. But does such a thing as the perfect blowjob exist, and if so, can such skills could be taught in a class? Would I become the Zamfir of the skin flute, or would I fail to make beautiful music on my lover's organ?

Like the surfers searching for the perfect wave in *Endless Summer*, my quest for perfection took me far from home. The seminar was held on the Upper West Side, a good ten subway stops from my apartment. Hesitantly, I approached the building, which purportedly housed something called the "Sexy Spirits Lecture Room." I had expected a scholarly stone palace bespeaking secret orders, but this looked more like an apartment complex.

Inside, a mustachioed man greeted me and requested that I remove my shoes before entering the space. A handful of women hovered in the doorway, slipping off their heels and glancing around furtively. I shared a nervous glance with a professional-looking woman. "I'm just gonna stay out here and wait for my friend," she said. Suddenly I felt like a loser for being there alone. It was high school all over again! I glanced over my shoulder to make sure no one had taped a "Kick me, I'm an art fag!" sign onto my back.

The lecture room screamed New Age aesthetics. Billowy wall hangings depicted Hindu goddesses, while a trippy, fractal video played to the rhythm of chanting Eastern music.

I introduced myself to Moxie, the evening's educator. "Hi, I'm Jen, the writer from Nerve who contacted you," I said, shaking her hand.

"So, what kind of stuff do you write about?" she asked.

"I'm writing the 'I Did It for Science' column that Grant Stoddard used to write. This is only my second installment."

"Oh, I looooved his column," she gushed.

To make a *Three's Company* analogy, I was starting to feel like Grant was the Suzanne Somers of Nerve, which made me the Jenilee Harrison of Nerve, which is a very tough thing to be, especially because most people don't even remember who Jenilee Harrison is.

Settling onto a rattan stool, I gazed at my new professor. An attractive brunette dressed modestly in black slacks and a blouse, she seemed to be in her mid-thirties. Nothing about her shouted "Blowjob Queen." The way she moved was tomboyish, like a much hotter version of my high school field hockey coach. I checked out Moxie's lips; they were larger than mine. She looked like a regular woman, yet apparently she held the key to pussy-whipping the male species.

Who is the typical blowjob student? I wondered, surveying the crowd. The average female student seemed to be in her thirties. When I mentioned this to Bruce, he postulated that many of these women were looking to "make a baby" and therefore felt they needed to acquire certain skills to make a man consider filling their hot ovens of ova. For whatever reason, thirty-something women are most interested in giving great head. (Men, mull this over the next time you drool over Reagan-era hotties.)

The male students seemed a bit older, probably in their forties. Most were wearing suits, and all gave off a distinct air of awkward straightness. Why would straight men attend a class on fellatio? Maybe to be in a room full of women who not only give blowjobs but want to improve their blowjobs, too.

With the exception of a hippie girl sitting on the floor and me, most students looked like they'd come from work on Wall Street.

Two suit-clad men sat down next to me. "What brings you here?" one of them asked me.

"I'm a sex columnist," I replied, regretting the words the second they came out of my mouth. The term "sex columnist" would seem to imply that I am some sort of expert on sex, which I'm not, so I added, "But I give horrible head."

"How does one become a sex columnist? I mean that's not really something you plan to do when you're seven."

"When I was seven, I wanted to be Miss America," I said, "but then I realized all of the Miss Americas had big boobs, and that didn't work out so well."

Another dude sat down next to me. I could hear him breathing in a manner I found irritating. "Should be an interesting night," he chortled.

Once almost thirty people had taken seats, Moxie began her lecture.

"Anyone here go to Catholic school?" she asked. A few hands shot up. Moxie explained that she was the daughter of an extremely traditional Sicilian Catholic father who taught her one thing about sex: it was for marriage and procreation only. I could not relate. Even though my parents never talked about sex, I had discovered their hidden copy of *The Joy of Sex* and often replicated the positions assumed by the bearded man and full-bushed woman with my Barbie dolls. Because I only had one Ken, there was a lot of wild lesbian activity rocking the Dream House.

"I never knew how to flirt," Moxie shared. "I never knew that it was okay to talk about sex." Until one fateful day, when she went off to college and started dating "Robert," the campus stud, who asked her, "Do you know what the perfect blowjob is?" This Yoda of fellatio then taught Moxie how to properly handle his lightsaber, and when she was done, he announced, "That's the best blowjob I've ever had," instilling his pupil with a sense of confidence and power.

"Sexual confidence is about power," Moxie told us. "Not dominance, but the power to express your needs and desires."

I'm confident that I'm good at some things, like making ribbon barrettes and swimming. But sexual confidence eludes me. The many years I spent being called "sweathog" and "fat-head" by my older brothers dealt a horrible blow to my confidence, as did the fact that I looked like the singer Meat Loaf for the first six years of my life.

Moxie asked the class to shout out qualities they thought were sexy. Curvy, stylish, smart, funny, and creative were among the responses. "Sexy is not an aesthetic," she said. "It's an aura."

Now that the class had been invited to shout things out, the "interrupters" began their running commentary. Every class, staff meeting, or rehearsal has at least one interrupter. These people won't let the teacher get a word in edgewise as they spout off nonsense that they imagine is somehow useful to the student body. These people will drive you insane. First the hippie girl on the floor began. Soon thereafter, the "breather" next to me was interjecting. I wrote in my notebook, *For the love of God, zip it and let's get on with the bj techniques.*

"We're getting off subject," Moxie said calmly. "Let's get back on track. How many people came here to learn oral sex techniques?"

Hands shot up. Moxie pulled out a Sharpie and wrote on a dry erase board: *Don't do it if you don't wanna.* This first step seemed easy enough. If I'm attracted to someone, I'll want to blow him, unless I have a sore throat or he has a wretched case of ball-sack odor.

Step two was also relatively simple: Always lubricate the shaft, as men chafe easily and you won't want to blow him if his penis is covered in flaking scabs of dry skin. Moxie professed that flavored lube is her fave. The male interrupter—who I was now convinced was actually a virgin—interjected, "Lube is too sticky," as if the entire class were planning on blowing him after the lecture.

We moved on to the subject of teasing. "Don't go right into it," Moxie suggested. "Tease him. Trail your hair along his inner thighs. Look into his eyes. Take the time to turn him on." So the idea is not to just drop to your knees and start munching on his cock, although sometimes that's called for if you're in a bar bathroom. However, I'd like to publicly state that I have a small bladder, and I think bar bathrooms should be used for three things: peeing, puking if necessary, and for writing flattering graffiti about me.

"Now it's time to get to work," Moxie declared. "But if you love doing it, it won't feel like work." Because I'd already reviewed several books on the subject of lovemaking, I already knew which "parts" supposedly produce a wellspring of love mayonnaise when properly handled. She suggested making a ring with your hand and placing it around the shaft while you move your lips, in order to cover more ground area.

"And, while you're doing it, don't forget to breathe!" she exclaimed. Apparently, breathing makes it easier not only to stay alive but to suck dick as well!

"Don't forget the boys!" Moxie advised. "But again, do it gently." The idea is not to bite into his chewy center, but to lick the salty coating.

"Change your pace. Don't let him come right away," she offered. "But when you get there, ladies, you have to tell him if you don't want him to come in your mouth."

So how do you know he's ready to shoot his load if he doesn't scream, "I'm going to come"? Most likely his breathing will get quicker and harder and his testicles will turn to walnuts, at which point it's time to make the big decision: to spit or to swallow? My feeling is that if you like someone enough to take his penis into your mouth for a prolonged period of time while also licking his balls and maybe even sticking a finger or a butt-plug up his ass, and you know that this person is disease-free, you might as well swallow. It's a great way to get some protein if you're a vegetarian. However, if the person you are blowing is a bad person, quickly move your head out of the way and see where his jizz lands. Then hand him a roll of Bounty and leave the room.

"Do you know why men prefer women to swallow?" Moxie asked. A handful of responses echoed throughout the classroom.

"They don't wanna make a mess and have to clean it up."

"My boyfriend tells me he feels abandoned if I don't."

"Because it feels good for him."

Moxie told us that it was all of these reasons and more: the physical aspects, the mental aspects, and the laziness.

"I hate it," one woman exclaimed. "It's like the texture of egg yolks!"

Others offered reasons why they either liked drinking semen or didn't. I felt like I was at a wine tasting.

"My test for any man," said a gorgeous Latina, "is whether or not he'll give me an open-mouthed kiss afterward. If he won't—goodbye."

"You're gonna lose a lot of guys that way," forewarned the breather. He then delivered a monologue wherein he theorized that homophobia made men afraid to kiss women who've just swallowed their jizz.

"But if men could blow themselves, they would, all day long," I told the interrupter. "And they would swallow."

"Civilization would die out if men could blow themselves," a man in the corner offered.

Chaos ensued as the class discussed a mythical world in which men could blow themselves.

"Okay, I have a question for the ladies," the male interrupter declared.

"As long as it's appropriate and respectful," Moxie stated, and I could feel a collective female eye-roll travel around the room like fans doing the wave at a Yankees game.

"If a woman goes down on you, does she always want reciprocation?"

"It's safe to say," I began, "that most women like cunnilingus, and that most women want to have orgasms. The answer to that question is yes. I have given hundreds of blowjobs," I declared. This is true. Considering I've been giving them for fifteen years, at roughly one a week, that totals 788 blowjobs. "And the number of times I've been orally pleased is nowhere near that." Now I was getting angry. "I once asked one of my lovers why he didn't go down on me as often as I went down on him, and he said it's because I DIDN'T ASK!" At this, the women were horrified, on the verge of rioting. "Communication is important in sex, but a woman shouldn't have to ask to have her pussy eaten every time, especially when it's already been determined that she likes it."

The class agreed. Reciprocation is humane.

"Does anyone have any questions?" Moxie asked.

"How do you feel about props like Altoids and honey?" I inquired. The men in the room quickly debunked the Altoid theory, explaining that an Altoid-coated tongue can often cause a tingling that is too intense. But an inventive class member noted success when she only used a sliver of an Altoid and some ice. Most of the class members seemed to think that honey was too messy and that anything you need a tarp for should be avoided.

After answering a few more questions, Moxie wished us luck in our cocksucking endeavors. Some of the student body mingled, but I shot out the door. Taking the class was only half of the lab. I would now have to blow someone. After all, you don't know if a driving class has worked until you get behind the wheel.

Originally, I thought I'd try out what I learned on Nick. He was my only lover at the time and the only man who'd ever complained about my fellatio techniques, specifically my inability to deep-throat his humungous penis like the many drag queens who'd blown him in the '80s.

But Nick and I had gotten into an argument and weren't speaking, a common occurrence at the time. It was impossible to get along with him, not just because he had the nerve to complain about my blowjobs, but also because he complained about everything, from the thread count of my sheets to my body shape. He liked big girls. I'm not big. He didn't like freckles. Freckles cover my entire body. He liked trashy-looking girls. I look like the girl next door. He didn't like the crumbs in my bed, yet he sat up in my bed, eating Cheetos, on my shitty sheets, in between opening his mouth to bitch and moan.

I called Tom.

"I'm depressed," I moaned. "I need to give someone a blowjob, and Nick is being a jerk."

"I can't believe he's being mean after you just took that class. If I had a girlfriend who took that class, I would be sooo nice to her."

"Exactly."

I went to the Anti-Slam that night and announced that I needed a lab partner.

My octogenarian friend, Leonard, offered to help. "I had my prostate removed," he declared, "so there's no chance I'll get anything on you." For a moment I considered it, but my ageist tendencies prevented such a hook-up.

"A blowjob really is a gift, when you think about it," Bruce suggested. "You should only blow someone nice."

Sex should never be considered a commodity, but Bruce was right. Only nice people deserve blowjobs.

I scanned the room, looking for that special someone.

"Fridate!" a performer named Orion called out. I had almost forgotten the "date" I'd made to hang out with Orion and his roommate, Erin, that Friday night.

Orion, a bi-curious man, and Erin, a lesbian, were the sole members of the self-professed shittiest band ever, Skrit Steak and the English Mufkins. They'd been coming to my open mike for a little over a month. In that time I'd seen them destroy a My Little Pony with a hammer, drink douche, and try to piss their pants onstage. About the only thing they hadn't done was play music. They were both in their early twenties, and cute.

Orion looked like Elijah Wood with a Mohawk. Though our original plans had been platonic, not fellatio-oriented, the thought of slipping his baggy trousers below his nubile hipbones and blowing him made me feel like a cross between a dirty old woman and Gandalf. And I liked the feeling. I had never been with a younger man.

He would be the first of many.

Friday afternoon, Erin and Orion sent me an email:

> We think we have fallen deeply in love with you.
> We couldn't help it.
> We think it's your eyes/ears/hair/mouth/arms/legs/
> vaginalarea/nose/smell/legs/your nips/stomach/heart/
> soul/voice/rev jenn jr/endospical research/tumor/
> See you tonight. We have pissed our beds for 4 straight
> nights about this.

When "Fridate" rolled around, the duo arrived at my love pad carrying a bag of beer and the board game *Girl Talk: The Game of Truth or Dare*, which is intended for 'tweens but can also be played by adventurous adults. *Girl Talk* consists of a small wheel that can be spun, *Price is Right*-style, to reveal questions and dares. An example of a dare would be, "Call the operator and ask for the President's phone number." A truth might be, "Did you ever cheat on a test?"

When *Girl Talk* is combined with alcohol, it can lead to heated situations. When Orion received a dare that requested he "borrow some clothing from an adult and wear it for the rest of the game," I lent him a negligee. When I was told to "do whatever the player to your left tells you to," Orion had me make out with both him and Erin. Soon I noticed that the *Girl Talk* wheel was being manipulated in order to create pornographic situations.

Seven hours, two pitcher-sized margaritas, one six-pack of Budweiser, two forties of Coors, and two tallboys of Bud later, we wound up at Erin and Orion's place, where we engaged in a raucous game of Seven Minutes in Heaven. As Erin passed out on the couch, Orion and I went way over the allotted seven minutes. "We're totally breaking the rules," I said, dropping to my knees and preparing to put what I'd learned to the test.

At first, I tried to concentrate on the various steps, announcing them as I went along. "Now I'm teasing you," I said, trailing my hair across his chest.

But my running commentary ended as I got to work licking, flicking my tongue, and sucking, whereupon Orion elicited several extremely grateful moans, which would have made my alma mater proud.

"Oh God, I want to fuck you," he pleaded. I, too, wanted the main course, but I remembered the assignment at hand and kept going, torturing both of us. I was so wet that I had to masturbate while blowing him, which prevented me from fully using my hands—probably a technical no-no. This, coupled with my intoxication, made for a blowjob that didn't reflect my recent education.

As 4 AM crept up and I was still going to town, sleep-deprivation-induced madness and fatigue took hold. To be honest, I have no idea how long I spent on my knees. We were in a time warp, and I was delirious. Orion was clearly deriving pleasure from the skills I'd learned. But I felt like Frodo right before he tosses the ring into the Cracks of Doom. My mind and body had been ravaged by exhaustion and debauchery, and I just couldn't go on. If I hadn't grown lazy and stopped, my techniques might have resulted in a protein shake for breakfast.

Succeeding in any field of study is a big commitment. At four in the morning, my commitment had waned. Had I not been inebriated, exhausted, and worried about breaking the rules of Seven Minutes in Heaven, I might have achieved greatness in the field of cocksucking. Instead, I failed in almost every capacity.

Even though I showed up for class on time and took abundant notes, it wasn't enough. My own personal lethargy prevented me from finishing what I started. This was as if, in painting *Woman with a Water Jug*, Vermeer had only painted the water jug. According to the feedback I got from Orion the following day, the skills I had acquired in class were apparent, but the dedication to excellence wasn't.

7 THE FACE OF GOD

"THE PROBLEM WITH making a sex tape," Kat said, "is that someone, somewhere, will see it—whether you like it or not."

"Yes, but I have nothing to lose," I argued. "I live in a sixth-floor walkup with a hole in the ceiling. I don't have a bank account or a working fridge. A sex tape can only help. Look at Paris Hilton. Now she has a hit TV show."

"But she started out famous."

"Well, maybe it can work in reverse. Also, it's not like I'm going to forget to label the tape."

I have no idea why so many people—especially celebrities—don't label their sex tapes. If I tape an episode of *The Golden Girls*, I'm going to label it, so I'm sure as hell going to label a tape of me bent over and taking it in my love-hole. Of course, I'm not going to label it "Me Fucking." Better to go with something more banal, like "Kevin Costner's *Waterworld*."

This precaution aside, Kat was right. Sex tapes always get

out. Even if you have been married to a person for fifty years and you think that person would never sell your tape to Rick Salomon for a million dollars, you are wrong. The simple act of being filmed in such a compromising position means there is a real chance someone other than you or your partner will see it.

But great achievements involve great risk. And considering I'd been making movies, albeit extremely low-budget movies, for most of my adult life, it seemed fitting that I combine my love of filmmaking with my new career as a sexual explorer.

When I suggested the home sex video idea to Ada, she had an intern burn me a compilation CD. "We didn't include the Fred Durst one. It stays with you," she shivered, a pallor crossing her face, "in a really bad way."

That night, I settled in to watch the Paris Hilton, Pam and Tommy, and Jenna Lewis tapes all in one sitting. Several hours of mind- and vagina-numbing footage later, my competitive spirit was ignited. "I can do better than this," I thought. While Tommy Lee and Pamela are jackable, I couldn't tolerate Tommy's trite banter and his need to begin every sentence with the word "fuck." (As in, "Fuck, I love you so much," and "Fuck, you are so gorgeous.") Sure, there's no way I'll ever look like Pamela Anderson naked, and I don't have access to fancy locations like penis-steered boats or lavish hotel rooms, but in the dialogue and creativity departments, I was way ahead of the game.

I asked some friends if they had ever taped themselves doing it, and if so, what the results were. "Nobody needs to see their own ohgod face," theorized my friend Lucky Dave. "That's the property of the person who gives it to you."

"I was mostly self-conscious about looking good on camera," said Tom. "And the subsequent viewing was much better than the actual production. A few days after Patti broke up with me and moved out, I figured I would bust out the tape and soothe my broken heart. It was thirty minutes of white noise. She'd erased the whole thing. She wouldn't even leave me that."

None of my friends could claim a truly happy experience. Nonetheless, I was determined to forge onward.

I called Nick. We were getting along well enough that I figured he'd be game.

Perhaps it would be considered cheating to make a home sex video with a director who has been making movies for twenty years, but it's also cheating to wear perfectly applied makeup and to cast a former Abercrombie & Fitch model as your costar, which is exactly what Jenna Lewis did on her tape.

"I'll do it, but no one can ever see it," he agreed.

"Of course no one will ever see it. I'll label it."

That seemed to be all the assurance Nick needed.

"Listen, I don't want it to be boring," I said. "Maybe it should have a plot. Or do you think then it becomes too much like amateur porn?"

"What's the difference?"

"I think amateur porn is made to be seen. And home sex videos are made only for the people who make them."

"Still, we could have a plot," Nick said. "I could play a man who lost his original penis due to leprosy, but just had a penis transplant and wants to try it out."

"I don't want it to be revolting. Plus, I think that plot is too convoluted."

Already we were engaged in the same director versus writer argument we'd been having for years.

"Maybe we could incorporate the giant plastic frog in your kitchen," Nick suggested.

"You can play a lab scientist who turns the frog into a woman who turns out to be a nymphomaniac, played by me. It's perfect."

He agreed to acquire a video camera and meet me the following Thursday, boner in hand. I hung up and set to work storyboarding, using the *Kama Sutra* as a guide.

Nick arrived Thursday, carrying a tripod, a bag of dirty magazines, and a camera. He plunked the case down on the kitchen floor and pulled out a camera the likes of which I hadn't seen since roughly 1980.

"It's the size of a mini-fridge!" I gasped. "Is it a Beta? Where did it come from?"

"Victor found it in a garbage can in Queens."

"Are you sure it works?"

Nick assured me it worked as he hauled the behemoth piece of history into my bedroom. He turned the RCA DP3's monitor toward us. "That's so we can watch what we're doing."

Taking a deep breath, I squeezed into my orange, fringed bathing suit. We placed my plastic bullfrog in the middle of my bed and recorded it as I narrated. "Late at night at the lab," I began, "and the professor is doing an experiment on a frog. What will happen?" This was the only dialogue I bothered to write for the video. I figured the rest would write itself.

We shut the video camera off, and I lay down in the frog's place. I looked at myself in the monitor, then opened my bedroom curtains just a bit until the lighting was flattering. Earlier I had noted that Pam and Tommy were smart to use natural light, the kindest of all lights—much better than the *Robocop* night vision employed by Rick Salomon in *One Night in Paris*.

I made a come-hither gesture to Nick. He hit the record button and joined me for a smooch. "Our collective pastiness will probably blind viewers," I noted, peeling off Nick's lab coat and unbuttoning his shirt.

"That camera is so loud," he groaned.

Indeed, the RCA DP3 sounded like a garbage disposal eating a box of nails—not the most erotic soundtrack in the world. I tried putting on music, but it just didn't fit. Some people make love to music, but Nick and I always fucked to total silence. It would have been dishonest to pretend otherwise.

With technical details resolved, we engaged in a round of tonsil hockey. As our clothes came off, we both turned toward the monitor repeatedly to see ourselves. I noticed Nick fixing his hair. It was sort of like talking to someone while you're wearing mirrored shades, and you realize the person's been staring at his own reflection the whole time.

Once we were thoroughly warmed up, I produced a condom and draped it over Nick's penis, setting a good example, should any promiscuous teens ever see our video. At this point, we were so aroused that the camera's significance began to pale.

I lay on my side, faced the camera and closed my eyes while Nick gently slid inside me. As I worked my fingers between my legs, my moaning grew loud enough to drown out the noisy camera. I must've been extremely turned on, because I came faster than a sixteen-year-old boy with a stack of *Juggs*. Once I caught my breath, Nick rolled on top of me and came moments later.

"I suppose I should hit pause," I sighed, not wanting to waste one minute of tape on the resolution phase.

Once we collected ourselves, it was time for my masturbation scene. Nick hoisted the ninety-pound camera from its tripod and directed the lens at my vulva as I busied myself with volume thirty-four of *Adam* magazine.

"This camera has some special effects," Nick noted, pressing a mysterious, unmarked button. "I think this one is some sort of mirror effect." He moved the camera in closer. "Wow—this is amazing! You've got to see this!"

He flipped the monitor over, and I marveled at the image. The mirror effect had multiplied my one humble vagina into two connected vaginas.

"That's awesome!" I exclaimed, inserting three fingers, which were thereupon doubled. Suddenly it looked as though fingers were growing out of me. "It's like a Georgia O'Keefe," I gasped. "It's the coolest thing ever."

"I feel like I'm seeing the face of God," I stated simply, unable to tear my eyes away from the glowing multilayered, finger-sprouting orifice that apparently belonged to me. "I don't know if I can come again. It's almost like it's not even me masturbating. It's some cubist version of me. Wait, I should put some lipstick on. Can you pause it?"

Nick paused the camera as I applied pink lipstick and searched for my vibrator. Vibrator in hand, I returned to my mark and recommenced the action. I closed my eyes, blocked out the kaleidoscopic image on the monitor, and came again, rolling my head back.

"Why don't you hold the camera and get a crazy POV shot while I blow you?" I suggested. "But be careful. That camera's really heavy. It might not be easy."

Sure enough, while I did my best to solicit a money shot, Nick's arm grew weak. He placed the camera next to the bed.

As I fellated Nick, I couldn't help but look into the monitor. My black eyeliner was smudged, and my tangled black hair was matted to my sweaty forehead. I looked like a cross between a malnourished, C-list porn star suckin' dick for a fix and Alice Cooper after a live concert. For a good 90 percent of the scene, I was doing what every female porn star does: looking directly into the camera. "I'm really not getting enough sleep," I thought.

After an extended session of sucking and jacking, Nick delivered a money shot that landed somewhere between my lips and my left cheekbone, creating a flattering dewy effect on my skin.

We turned the DP3 off and lay in total silence for at least two minutes before clamoring to view the tape's contents.

When Nick popped the tape into my VCR, my heart sank: the image was scrambled. Of course—there had to be a reason someone would throw out such an amazing camera. The RCA DP3 had eaten our tape, and we'd have to start the whole experiment over from scratch! The face of God I'd seen in my multiple vaginas was lost forever, a cruel trick of technology!

"Maybe we should try syncing it up to Pink Floyd's 'Dark Side of the Moon,'" I suggested.

"Try the tracking button."

With bated breath, I held down the tracking button. Slowly the picture became visible.

While I've seen myself nude in photographs, I had never seen myself having sex. I fully expected to be disgusted by the sight of my naked flesh bouncing up and down. But in the natural light, I almost looked like a person who exercises. I wasn't mortified, but I thought I looked small and asexual. In the long shots it was almost impossible to decipher whether Nick was fucking a man or a woman.

"My orgasm seemed fake," I noted.

"It wasn't?" Nick asked, surprised.

"I wonder if this would turn anyone on. Are you turned on?" I asked.

"No, are you?"

"No."

We perked up during the distorted, split-beaver masturbation scene where I appeared to be a many-armed, many-vagina-possessing, multiorgasmic, glowing goddess of love.

Upon ejecting the tape, Nick produced a Sharpie and labeled it "The Face of God." Neither of us was wet, hard, or otherwise turned on. If the goal was to make a red-hot, amateur porno, we failed. However, through a total accident involving an abandoned camera from an earlier decade (which may or may not have been left in a trashcan by a deity or alien) for about ten minutes of videotape, we made art.

After the initial viewing, Nick went home, and I watched the tape a few more times for research purposes until I noticed the tape was growing more scrambled with each viewing. While other people joke about destroying their sex tapes after making them, it seemed ours would self-destruct if viewed again. I didn't show the sex tape to anyone else, even for a reaction. I didn't want to weird out my friends or, even worse, bore them. Showing your home sex video is sort of like showing your friends pictures of your summer vacation: they probably don't want to see it.

8   BALLOONAUT

BETWEEN WORKING AT the bookstore, hosting the open mike, making movies, and writing a column, I didn't have much free time. And what spare time I had was spent surfing the web trying to figure out what to write about next. I was developing carpal tunnel looking at weird porn sites when I stumbled upon the wackiest fetish I'd ever heard of: *balloons.*

I couldn't believe that in this epoch of double-anal and bukkake people were getting off on balloons. In my eyes, balloons were simply colorful pieces of plastic that evil clowns occasionally fashioned into animal shapes. I was intrigued.

I Googled the words "balloon fetish." Several links to websites appeared, along with one link to *Balloon Farm,* a 1999 film starring Rip Torn. Balloon fetishists, I learned, are called "looners." Most of the looner sites comprised relatively softcore material featuring pretty young women blowing up, squeezing, and sitting on balloons. Many presented warnings before "popping content" was displayed. Herein, I learned of the two distinct looner categories: poppers and nonpoppers. Poppers obviously dig popping, and nonpoppers are more aroused by the inflated balloon in all its glory.

I asked friends if they knew anything about looners.

"Oh, yeah, I saw that once on HBO," said my friend Amy.

"Wow, they probably worship the Michelin Man," said my friend Mark, incredulous.

My friend John theorized that the entire fetish originated with a *Super Friends* episode titled "The Balloon People."

Everyone I spoke to either had no reliable information or had never heard of a balloon fetish.

I continued my quest for knowledge online, where I searched for balloon fetish activities in the greater metropolitan area. After stumbling upon a New York City fetish calendar, I noticed a balloon party scheduled for that very weekend. It was listed as part of the Baroness' Fetish Retinue, a monthly party held at an East Village bar. This wasn't the first time I'd heard of the Retinue. The previous month, Erin and Orion had naively and drunkenly wandered in, whereupon the Baroness whipped Erin's ass until it was redder and more swollen than a Hamadryas baboon's in heat. Since then, she'd developed a huge crush on the Baroness.

I emailed the Baroness, requesting more information about the balloon party, specifically whether there was a dress code. Do people dress in balloons? I wondered. The last thing I wanted was to be ostracized for dressing inappropriately.

The following day, the Baroness returned my email. She explained that partygoers sometimes climbed inside balloons. There would also be balloon bondage and anything else she could come up with. "As far as a dress code," she shared, "the price of admission depends on what you wear: it's free if you're fabulous, $5 in fetish, $15 in all black, and $20 in streetwear. If you were to come covered in balloons, the door bitch might think you were fabulous. But she's very particular."

I called my friend Claudia, a lawyer and uptown girl who rarely gets to engage in anything truly deviant. "Do you want to go to a balloon fetish party with me tomorrow night?" I inquired.

"Balloon fetish?" she repeated.

"People get off on blowing up balloons and popping them, and that kind of thing. It'll be fun."

"It's not going to be an orgy or anything?"

"No. It's very G-rated. It's balloons."

"Okay, I'll go. But I'll meet you beforehand. I'm not going alone."

I invited a few other friends, including Erin and Orion.

On Sunday night, I donned my thigh-high gold boots, a powder-blue mini-dress, and eyelashes the size of caterpillars, hoping the door bitch would deem me fabulous. Upon our arrival, Claudia and I were surprised to find that the door bitch was not the six-foot-tall drag queen we'd expected, but a tiny man with a brazen stare. Nevertheless, we were proclaimed fabulous and granted admittance.

"Looks like a swingin' sausage party," I said, surveying the overwhelming ratio of men to women. A guy with a luscious mane of ass hair sauntered by in a thong. Another man with long blond hair had gone the opposite route: he wore a full-body PVC catsuit.

"How do you get into that?" I asked him.

"Two ways: you can soak it in water, or you can use baby powder."

"Looks good," I told him, glancing around the room.

People who looked like they'd just left their temp jobs mingled with people who looked like they'd spent hours getting ready. Latex was the overwhelming fashion choice. A green balloon floated in front of us, and Claudia joyfully stomped on it. A man blowing up a balloon in the corner shot us a nasty look, while another man sighed, "You can do that again." Clearly, there was tension between poppers and nonpoppers. Would there be a dance-off? Already things were exciting. I whipped out my notepad.

A bespectacled, preppy-looking man approached us and introduced himself as Clay.

"How did you find out about this?" Claudia asked him.

"I'm on an email list for this fetish," he replied.

Thrilled to meet an actual looner, I asked, "Is it the balloons themselves? Or is it the pretty girls blowing them up? Or is it the pretty girls popping them?"

"Well, I'm not really into the popping. Some people are all about the popping. They're just like, 'Blow it up and pop it already, damn it!' But I'm more into the sensual aspects of it—the way it feels when it's inflated. I still like sex, and I still like women. Balloons just add a little something extra."

"Do you think I'm dressed appropriately?" I asked.

"Well, you could have dressed as a balloon delivery-woman," he suggested.

Our chat was interrupted by a commotion at the door. Erin and Orion, both covered from head to toe in balloons, were arguing with the door bitch.

"What's wrong?" I asked, coming to their aid.

"He says we're not in fetish gear," Erin moaned. "He wants to charge us twenty bucks apiece!"

"They're totally in fetish gear," said Clay. The door bitch just shook his head. Apparently, to him, only latex and leather qualified. The possibility of a new genre threw him for a loop.

Defeated, Erin and Orion walked out. "We're gonna go to Benny's Burritos and see what happens," they said. The door bitch magically had a change of heart and let them in for ten. Once inside, they began to hug everyone in the room.

"Wow, there are a lot of pant-tents being pitched right now," I whispered to Claudia.

As I mingled with the crowd, I collected email addresses from people who claimed to be looners. Several were happy to share their insights with me. I learned that most balloon fetishists enjoyed playing with balloons before they were consciously sexual.

Some feared the popping noise but later eroticized it. One looner told me he was influenced by the early-'70s game show *Beat the Clock*, which featured leggy models performing stunts that involved balloons. It wasn't too hard to see how a young mind could make the connection.

The Baroness finally arrived, wearing a latex dress of her own design. She announced that the party had officially started, then beckoned Erin to the stage, where she wordlessly instructed her to stand in the corner and produced a whip. Then, like Legolas slaying Orcs with his arrow, the Baroness deftly obliterated each balloon on Erin's body until there was nothing left but stubs of torn latex dangling from safety pins.

Once both Erin and Orion had been stripped of their balloons, a balloon-oriented performance began. It involved a woman with vampire fangs clad in a salmon-colored latex catsuit, a man drinking a martini, and a pigtailed woman in a schoolgirl outfit being bound at her wrists and ankles by long balloons. The plot had something to do with a lost pet, and the martini-drinking man made a balloon dog for the fanged woman—not an easy task. There's a reason clown college is harder to get into than Harvard.

The Baroness soon informed me that the giant balloons were going to be blown up shortly, and I was slated to go second.

"Rev., what if it deflates and you start to suffocate?" fretted Claudia.

I hadn't thought about the actual physics of it.

"That would be the coolest way to die ever!" Erin exclaimed.

"It would make the cover of the *Post*, that's for sure," I mused. "My poor parents would be so humiliated. I wish there were EMTs on hand."

"I'll get a knife, so I can cut you out if I have to," said Claudia, looking around the room for a weapon.

"Just use your keys," I said, feeling my knees quiver like a deep-sea diver's.

Onstage, the balloon operator, a burlesque performance artist named BALLOONHEDZ, was making preparations. Apparently putting people in balloons takes more planning than a space-shuttle launch. The stage was thoroughly dusted, and a gray blanket was laid across the floor to ensure that no antimatter would burst the balloon. As the expectant crowd gathered around, a giant Shop-Vac hose was wheeled onstage.

Nena's "99 Red Balloons" played as BALLOONHEDZ began to inflate the first giant balloon. Appropriately enough, it was red. I climbed onstage and watched up close as Amalie, a "balloonaut" clad in a fierce latex mini-dress, prepared to dive in.

"Put your hands in front of your face and make a point," the Baroness coached from the sidelines. BALLONHEDZ then removed the Shop-Vac hose from the balloon, revealing an opening the size of a rabbit hole, which Amalie was to squeeze into. Physically, it seemed about as possible as squeezing toothpaste back into the tube. "Go! Go! Go!" the audience cheered as the Baroness gave Amalie a shove. But just as soon as Amalie's body disappeared into the balloon, the whole thing popped, and the aspiring balloonaut lay awkwardly in a pool of deflated latex. The audience sighed with disappointment.

I was next. My nerves rattled. I felt like a contestant on *Fear Factor* who was about to eat a maggot-filled doughnut. "Take notes," I said, handing my pen and notebook to Erin. "Orion, hold my purse. Claudia, have your keys ready. I'm goin' in!"

A large, leather-clad guy who looked like the cartoon version of Batman introduced himself as Morpheus. He asked if I was nervous.

"Yeah, I'm worried I'll pop it," I said. "Or that I won't, and it'll be claustrophobic and I'll freak out."

"Don't be nervous. Just think of it as a soft, womblike experience."

"How do I not pop it?"

"The first girl popped it because she was wearing too many clothes."

"Are you saying I should get naked?"

"It'd be a lot easier."

I approached the Baroness. "Morpheus suggested I get naked. I think it's a good idea."

"We can't have you getting naked. That would be illegal, since we're in a bar," she said. "Although we could put black tape over your nipples." And with a deftness that would make MacGyver's head spin, the Baroness produced a roll of electrical tape. I followed her to the corner of the stage, where she unzipped my dress while murmuring a steady stream of instructions. "You must remove your jewelry and your shoes—anything that could pop the balloon. It's very important that you make a point with your hands. I'll give you a shove when it's time."

I pulled my dress off, revealing an embarrassing pair of turquoise $2 Kmart panties, which would surely be ridiculed by the latex divas surrounding me. The Baroness applied four tiny pieces of tape to my now-erect magic wands, ensuring my teats would be legal should the boob squad arrive.

I'm ready, I'm ready, I'm ready, I sang to myself, trying to channel the fearlessness of SpongeBob as I stepped in front of a massive green balloon. The crowd cheered.

There was no turning back, no room for failure. I would dive in as though my life depended on it, like C-3PO leaping into an escape pod. I knew this would not look pretty. It is impossible to look poised when diving into a giant balloon, clad only in a pair of skivvies and electrical tape. I'm sure I looked like a complete jackass as I dove toward the hole. Yet somehow I wriggled in with relative ease.

The inside of the balloon was much different from the outside. It was like being on the other side of the looking glass, a separate world. Sounds were muffled, and I was surrounded by bright green latex, which was growing larger by the second. The smell of rubber was overwhelming. I felt like I'd been miniaturized and dropped into an old-fashioned swim cap. I wasn't claustrophobic or scared, but I wasn't aroused either. Oceanic feelings overwhelmed me. I was serene and obscenely happy.

Like most people who haven't spent years in primal-scream therapy, my memories of the womb are buried under multiple layers of song lyrics and useless trivia. But I imagine that being in the womb rocked. I am told that I stayed in the womb far past my delivery date and when I did emerge, I attempted to greet the world ass first. It was if I couldn't bear the thought of actually seeing what was out there. (It could also have been the result of my mother riding the Teacups at Enchanted Forest Amusement Park to induce labor, but that's another story entirely.) Hence, it is pure speculation when I say that I felt like an overgrown fetus relishing the simplicity of intrauterine existence.

As the balloon stretched, it became less opaque, and the lights and people outside grew just barely visible. I began to wonder how long I could stay inside when, suddenly, the air hose became detached and the balloon started shrinking around me. Claudia was right: I was going to experience the most ridiculous death ever. But like Bowie's Major Tom, there was nothing I could do.

I think I heard someone say, "Oh shit!" In a second, the hose was reintroduced into the balloon's hole, and it reinflated, this time larger than before.

"Are you ready for some company?" a voice boomed from outside. "Make room."

I backed up and watched as a lithe young man named Michael dove through the opening. Witnessing this reverse-birth from the inside was even stranger than it had seemed on the outside. First I saw his head, then his torso, and then his whole body appeared. What do you say to someone you barely know, with whom you're suddenly half-naked in a balloon? "How's it goin'?" I asked, taking his hand and helping him up like a tour guide on another planet. His smile indicated pure joy.

He was now in on the secret: being inside a giant balloon is awesome. "Oh my God," he gasped.

"Do you feel like you're in deep space?" I asked.

"Yeah, this is amazing. I want to be naked too," he proclaimed, peeling off his latex trousers.

"It's definitely nicer being naked in here," I said. Not that I'd ever been clothed in a balloon, but the latex felt velvety and stretchy against my skin.

We stared at each other like we'd just climbed through a wardrobe and found Narnia. It was hard to believe the real world lay just outside the latex. We touched the balloon. We touched each other's hands. We knelt down, stood up, and pressed ourselves against the latex. Finally, Michael said, "Kiss me, Rev. Jen! We're in a balloon!" and we shared a celebratory kiss that no one in the audience was privy to.

Our peaceful floating continued for what seemed like hours, but was really only about five minutes. At that point, we were told to prepare for more company. There's not possibly enough room or oxygen for three people, I thought (although BALLOONHEDZ later told me he'd fit four women inside a balloon at once). We backed up and awaited the next visitor.

The hole opened. Amalie, the first balloonaut, was making a second attempt. This time she managed to wriggle all the way in, but almost as soon as she had, the balloon popped and we became a crumpled heap of latex-covered losers. Like coming out of anesthesia, it was a quick jolt back to crude reality. We stood up, and the crowd cheered as though we'd just scored a gold medal. Orion handed me my purse, and Erin handed me my notebook, which contained exactly three indecipherable sentences. "We need to discuss this," she said.

"Where are my clothes?" I asked.

"I almost used my keys," Claudia gasped. "I was so close to busting you out of there."

Once dressed, I went straight to the bar. I was no longer an overgrown fetus, and I needed a beer. The bartender presented me with a freebie as I sat down and took several deep breaths, relishing what little oxygen exists in crowded East Village bars. Around me, bacchanalia had erupted. Onstage, another overly dressed balloonaut had burst the last of the giant balloons. Morpheus had struck up a conversation with Claudia, who agreed to be spanked by his massive Batman arms. Two men had handcuffed Erin's wrists behind her back and were leading her around, feeding her sips of beer. "It's cool, man," she said, noticing my worried glance. "I'm getting a free drink out of this." Amalie was reclining on a sofa, having her toes sucked by a man in a thong. Three scantily clad women were onstage being tied to a giant phallic balloon and whipped by more balloons.

The overabundance of balloons and half-dressed, heavily made-up revelers made me feel as if I were at an after-hours circus in which the clowns were finally allowed to cut loose. Even the door bitch was smiling.

9   LIVE NUDE GIRL

KAT AND I attended a vampire fetish party at a warehouse in Brooklyn, hoping to meet bloodsucking freaks who might want to victimize me for science. What we found instead was a sprinkling of cape-clad dorks, discussing computer technology.

"I had a feeling," Kat said. "In nerd evolution, vampirism comes right after *Dungeons and Dragons*."

"This is all Anne Rice's fault."

My column was due in a week and I had to do something even if it meant letting a file clerk in prosthetic vampire fangs give me hickies.

As I made the rounds looking for that special Lestat, I ran into a performance artist friend named Velocity Chyaldd whom I hadn't seen in years. She was reclining naked in a bathtub full of stage blood while vampire nerds fawned over her.

Hers was the first vagina I ever licked, back when I was twenty-one and bi-curious.

"Rev.!" she exclaimed, climbing out of the tub and wrapping her bloody arms around me. "What are you doing here?"

I explained the situation.

"Why don't you become a stripper for your next column? It would be hilarious."

Stripping for science hadn't occurred to me, probably because "flat-chested," "pasty," and "Elvish-speaking" aren't qualities the general populace normally associates with strippers. And as for my dancing experience, it consisted of exactly one year of ballet at the age of six, which I abandoned to join an all-boys soccer team.

Despite all this, multiple viewings of *Flashdance* during my formative years left me with a secret yearning to become a stripper, if only for a day. Plus, I love attention, and being a stripper is a good way to get a lot of it.

Velocity continued, "I used to work at this all-nude club in Queens called Wiggles. You could totally get a job there."

I had the notion that the Giuliani administration had all but obliterated strip clubs from Gotham. It seemed that stripping had become a thing of the past, reduced to pole-dancing workout classes at Crunch, replaced with more artful burlesque shows. I was shocked to hear that an all-nude club existed within the five boroughs.

"I don't know, Velocity. Compared to most strippers, I'm geriatric."

"Dude, all you have to do is show up."

"Are you sure? I have small boobs."

"Trust me," she said slowly. "All you have to do is show up."

I was starting to get the impression that Wiggles was not the most high-end of establishments. My friend Victor later told me he once saw a stripper there accept a dollar bill using only her vaginal muscles. Maybe not high-end, but that's certainly a talented workforce.

"The first thing you need is a stripper name," Velocity told me. "I'm thinking you would make a good Trinity. It's innocent, but also a little freaky."

The religious connotations of that seemed pompous, so I asked friends for suggestions. Among their brainstorms were Hamburger McFlapsalot, Shecky Titsberger, Polaka Clitskowski, Clitsy McLabe, Carrie Bigpee, Coco, Georgina, Cozy, Misty, Windy, Jovi, Willa, Lickety Split, Fancy, Jean, Louis Elfesteem, and Benedicta (in honor of the new pope). After much consideration, I chose Trinity.

Velocity promised to teach me some basic moves, so the next day I went to her apartment. I'd never even been inside a strip club, so I had a lot of questions.

"First thing: you need stripper shoes. What size are you?" Velocity asked.

"Six and a half."

"Here. Try these on," she said, handing me the most daunting pair of hot-pink heels I'd ever seen. Stripper shoes perform several functions: they elongate the legs, flatten the stomach, and push the butt out. They also make it hard to walk three feet without falling on your ass. As I slipped them on, my body image issues were replaced with the very real fear that I would break both ankles.

"These shoes make you wanna take your clothes off!" said Velocity as I hobbled around her bedroom.

Once I had walking down, it was time for a dancing tutorial. My favorite dance music is that of Dave Clark Five and the Box Tops, but Velocity assured me these bands were not played in strip clubs. I would need more modern music, either hip-hop or rock. She put on a Massive Attack CD and, like Mr. Miyagi training the Karate Kid, she took me through a series of movements, pretending the posts of her canopy bed were poles.

"You'll see a lot of girls hump the poles," she said. "Sometimes they'll even slide the pole between their ass cheeks."

"Ew. Do they 409 the poles afterward?"

"Some girls do carry baby wipes onstage," she reassured me.

After I obediently humped the pole a few times, Velocity showed me how to remove my G-string without falling over or getting it tangled in my stiletto heels.

"Some girls like to get really dramatic, but you should keep it simple. Try this," she said. Leaning over and sticking her ass out, she pulled her panties off in one uncomplicated motion.

"Some girls get all crazy—yoga moves and stuff—but really, you should just take the thing off."

Those were the fundamentals. Now all I needed was a signature style. Velocity suggested that I emphasize my innocent appearance, but we both agreed the schoolgirl look had been done to death. She pulled out a baby-doll negligee set made of hot-pink lace. I tried it on. The skivvies rode high enough to reveal my ample ass cleavage. It was perfect. I chose to wear my hair in pigtails, reasoning that this always looks slutty on grown women. The entire getup reminded me of *Angel: High School Honor Student by Day. Hollywood Hooker by Night*.

A few days later, I called Wiggles. A man with a heavy Russian accent told me I could come in any time.

"Is tonight okay?"

"Any time," he repeated.

I called Velocity. "It's on," I said.

"It's Friday. It's a total frat-boy night. Are you sure you want to do it?"

"Oh my God. It's Friday the thirteenth!" I was suddenly horrified.

"Thirteen is a lucky number for witches," Velocity said excitedly. "You have to do it tonight. I'll go with you if you want."

"Oooh, pigtails," a man in a sweat-stained T-shirt gushed when Velocity picked me up at my apartment. I already felt violated, and I was still clothed.

"It just dawned on me," I told Velocity, "that in a few minutes, an entire roomful of people will see my vagina."

"Yeah, but it's a roomful of people who've been looking at nothing but vaginas for the past hour."

"So it's more like going to the gynecologist's office."

"Exactly."

This did little to quell my nerves. On the way to Wiggles, we stopped off at a bar. Two glasses of wine were hardly enough to stop my knees from shaking. I've never been good at job interviews, and this was going to be a rough one. Because Wiggles was a nonalcoholic club, I'd be dancing in front of sober people. I couldn't decide what would be scarier—dancing for rowdy drunks or people who might actually remember the night. I worried that I might see the mailman or the dude from the bodega. How would I ever explain?

Upon our arrival at Wiggles, a jovial Russian man named Ivan greeted us, and a burly bouncer asked for ID.

"Shit, I forgot mine," I said, rifling through my purse. "But look, I have crow's feet." I pointed to the fine lines around my eyes.

"Whenever you're ready, you can go on," Ivan assured me. Velocity ushered me to the dressing room, where a dozen strippers congregated in front of mirrors, applying makeup. The average age was about ten years my junior.

As I awaited my moment of truth, the girls backstage ignored me. In a matter of minutes, the DJ announced, "Trinity on standby." I left the dressing room and stood next to the stage. I really should have done more preparation, I thought, as I watched the girl before me effortlessly dangle upside down from the pole. I hadn't realized the Cirque du Soleil dancers spent their free time here.

I handed the DJ the Massive Attack CD I'd practiced to and told him to play track one, "Angel." Onstage, I awkwardly twirled around the poles and gyrated my hips. I tried to "breathe with my vagina," as Martha Graham purportedly instructed her dancers to do.

I became acutely aware of time and how I was going to spend it, wondering when I should take my negligee off and when the dollar bills would start coming. I felt a little bit like a hobo begging for change on the subway. Only I was begging for change half-naked, onstage in six-inch heels.

Despite this distracting introspection, I managed what I believe is a revolutionary act in a strip club: I smiled at the small group of customers before me. They responded by producing dollar bills, rolling them up, and slipping them into my G-string. Velocity held up a bill at the end of the stage and made a come-hither gesture. I waltzed over to her.

"Dude, take your panties off," she whispered, her voice quavering like a nervous stage mother's. "The second song's almost over!" I danced back out to center stage and managed to remove the G-string without inciting disaster. Upon the unveiling of my vulva, I received a few more bills. The third song was short, and before I knew it, my audition was over.

"Rev., your body looked amazing. You have great legs!" Velocity exclaimed as I got off the stage.

"Thank you. It's the only benefit of living in a sixth-floor walkup for ten years." I radiated a kind of body confidence I'd never known, one that must only come from dancing naked under the most flattering light possible and having people give you money for it.

Ivan approached. "Want to start Tuesday at eight?"

"Sounds good," I replied.

He handed me a business card that featured Wiggles' logo, a silhouette of a naked lady with "Wiggles" spelled out in cursive over her body. In the upper-right-hand corner was Wiggles' catchy slogan: "More than topless. We go one step beyond."

When Tuesday rolled around, I arrived at Wiggles, where another Russian man, Konstantin, addressed me sharply. "Will you be ready by eight?" he asked, looking me up and down.

"I'm ready now," I told him as I walked toward the back-stage area.

"Okay, if you're not ready by eight you get fined $10."

I nervously entered the dressing room, whereupon two strippers, Alexa, a lanky Russian blonde, and Roxy, a chubby brunette, shot me eye daggers. They totally ignored me, and I felt embarrassed for even being alive. As I sat down and reapplied my lip gloss, the two discussed a fellow dancer who had kicked a Wiggles patron in the head the previous evening after he tried to touch her vagina. After thoroughly exhausting this subject, they moved on to the topic of Sagittarius men being players. Having been taught astrology by Jackie Stallone, astrologer to the stars, I tried to chime in with my knowledge of Sagittarians. They turned and looked at me with silent disgust.

I shrank into my chair, realizing this was how every Linda Blair/women-in-prison movie started. Soon they'd be yanking on my pigtails and spitting at me. I perked up when a beautiful petite brunette in a black string bikini entered the room and sat down next to me. "Hi, I'm Lena," she smiled.

"Hi. I have magazines if you get bored," I said to her, handing her my new copy of *InStyle* and staring at her dewy twenty-something skin.

"Thanks."

"Trinity on standby," the DJ called out. As I turned the corner to leave the dressing room, I tripped over a step and had to hold myself up on a locker.

There were exactly three people in the audience: a couple deep in conversation and Bruce. I'd invited my closest friends to attend my stripping debut for moral support and protection, but Bruce had been the only one wealthy enough to swing the $10 cover charge and mandatory $2 coat-check fee.

"Thank you," I mouthed to him.

As the DJ played some Limp Bizkity-type music, which is all the craze with the young kids these days, I gyrated my hips and delivered my sauciest smile. I caught the attention of the male portion of the couple, but the woman seemed to think I was cockblocking her. He gestured toward me, but the woman shook her head. I shimmied to the ground and stretched out my garter-clad thigh to receive his dollar.

Then Bruce held out a dollar, and I sauntered over, crouching so we could talk.

"How long do you have to be here?" he asked.

"I don't know. I don't think I can stay. It's killing my soul."

"Yeah, it seems really horrible."

"Maybe you can facilitate my escape."

I danced away and looked at the couple, running my hands over my body in mock arousal. The man approached and slid another dollar under my garter, but as the third song began to play, the woman whispered something to him, and they got up and left. They didn't even stay long enough to see my vulva. How rude!

"I've totally failed," I said to Bruce. "I made them leave."

"They probably went home to bone," he assured me. "You were a lot better than the girl who was on before."

"I'm gonna get the hell out of here. Stay there, and I'll meet you in a second."

Backstage, Konstantin was sitting in the dressing room.

"So . . . how long is a shift?" I asked him.

"If you arrive at six, you stay till two. If you arrive at eight, you stay till four."

My mind did the math. I realized Konstantin expected me to work for eight hours. This was about seven hours too many.

"What if you have to leave?" I asked.

"We don't like girls to leave," he barked. "Not unless they're sick or have twisted an ankle."

This did not sit well with me. The second The Man tells me I can't do something, I want nothing more than to do it. I find confinement unbearable. I once walked out of a hospital with an IV dangling from my arm because I wanted a slice of pizza from the outside world. Images of John Dillinger carving a wooden gun in his cell sprang to mind. I had to find a way out. I'd sunk to depths of pure misery after only an hour.

When I emerged from the dressing room, Lena was dancing for two turkey-necked businessmen who were drinking from bottles of Poland Spring. She twirled her incredible body around the poles with unparalleled finesse. I imagined both men had boners, and I wondered whether it was strange for two straight men to sit side by side, sporting wood. Did they acknowledge each other's boner, or was it a silent understanding?

As Bruce and I discussed various methods of possible escape, Alexa approached us. She looked straight through me.

"You've been here before, no?" she said to Bruce.

"Nope, never been here," he replied.

"How would you like me to show you around?" (Translation: How would you like to spend all of your money receiving totally disinterested lap dances from me?)

"No, thank you."

"Come on. I'll show you around."

"No, really. Thank you, though."

"I don't bite!" she snapped, walking away.

"Wow, that was really rude," Bruce marveled.

"Yeah, she didn't even know you're just my friend. For all she knew, you were my customer. She was trying to steal my customer! That's it! Meet me outside in five minutes." I walked backstage and threw on my dress.

"Are you leaving?" asked Roxy, suddenly developing an interest in me.

"Nah, just going to smoke."

Pulling on my boots, I eyed my copy of *Uncut* featuring Jimmy Page on the cover, along with my new *InStyle*. I wanted to take them with me but figured it would arouse too much suspicion. They would be my gifts to Lena for being nice.

"Do you know how I get out of here to go smoke?" I asked a girl in a pink bikini.

"Yeah, follow me."

I followed her to a side exit, where she opened the door.

"Be careful," she said. "If the door closes, it'll lock behind you." Stepping outside, I realized she hadn't led me to an actual club exit, but to an enclosed alleyway with no exit. It was a pen for smoking strippers. My night at Wiggles had turned into *Escape from Alcatraz*. I eyed another entrance into the club and slipped into the hallway unnoticed. With the stealth of a ninja assassin, I crept down the hallway and made it out the door. Bruce was standing across the street, snapping photos. I called his name as I ran down the street. He caught up with me, and together we walked away from Wiggles as quickly as possible. We were both paranoid that Konstantin might run after me. Bruce even hallucinated a Russian army officer standing on the corner.

"There's gotta be a bar around here where we can hide," I stated, looking around.

A child of not more than ten overheard me and gave me a set of convoluted directions to a nearby bar, which he told me was "sort of retro but cool." We went off in search of beer and refuge. Finding none, we finally hopped on the subway, where we were offended by the very sight of the straphanger's poles.

"Thank God there's a seat," I sighed. "I won't be able to touch another pole for a week."

10 LOVE MAYONNAISE

I WAS STARTING to notice that Erin and Orion's free-spiritedness bordered on insanity. I worried that if they grew any more deviant, they would end up in jail.

My friend Brian told me he'd run into Erin on the street and she kicked him in the balls for no reason.

When I asked her why, she told me he "pissed her off."

At my open mike, their sets were becoming more horrifying. The bar almost cancelled my show when Erin vomited on Orion's nude chest. The following week, Erin stuck a tampon up Orion's ass.

I tried to explain to the bar owner that they were like the "American branch of the Vienna Actionists," only funnier.

They were also disease-free, attractive, and willing to participate in my experiments without asking for anonymity. They liked being "literary figures" and proudly posted links to my columns on their website.

At bars I made out with both of them. They called me their "slutty elf girlfriend."

In turn, my friends began calling them my "boyfriend and girlfriend."

What was odd about their relationship is that, though they fooled around with me, they didn't fool around with each other. They were roommates, best friends, and bandmates, but not lovers.

They were the perfect antidote to Nick, who had tried to control every aspect of my life. Skrit Steak had no desire to control me. Instead they wanted me to be out of control, like them.

They rang my buzzer at all hours.

"It's Erin and Orion. Can we come upstairs and pee on you?"

"No."

"Will you let us give you a bubble bath?"

"Okay."

Their weed dealer gave them porn, which we watched together on my bed. We engaged in frequent three-ways in which they both touched me but didn't touch each other.

For Orion's birthday, Erin announced they were throwing an Under the Sea–themed prom in their apartment. When I arrived for the prom, I noticed they'd taped an agenda to the door.

Two of the activities listed were "beer-pong" and "fucking a jar of mayonnaise."

Inside, they'd inflated 300 balloons, which took up all of the floor space of their tiny apartment. Orion had spent a week cutting sea creature shapes out of construction paper, and these were glued to one wall. Their bathtub or "lagoon" was full of dirty green water and streamers.

I was one of three guests. There was an open mike regular

named Drew, his hot nineteen-year-old prom date, and me. We sat down and played beer-pong, which was followed by a game of Seven Minutes in Heaven. After seven minutes in heaven, Orion announced that it was time for him to fuck a jar of mayonnaise.

Of the many condiments that disgust me, mayonnaise is at the top of the list. Part of me wanted to flee in horror.

"He needs a fluffer!" Erin insisted, looking at me.

I followed Orion to his bedroom where I gave him what he later said was an "incredible" blowjob.

Once he was hard, he journeyed into the living room pants-less. Erin handed him a massive open jar of mayonnaise that she had bought at the 99-cent store. It wasn't even brand-name.

He held the jar in both hands and thrust his penis into the revolting mixture.

We cheered him on as he boned the mayo for several minutes before finally realizing it was fruitless. The condiment just wasn't bringing him to orgasm.

Since I loathe mayo, I flatly refused to finish him off. He washed his penis and we commenced playing beer pong.

Though the event had been more interesting than my high school prom, I worried: *Had we all become too strange to have normal sex?* If I continued down this road, what perversities lay in store?

A year later Orion and I discussed the mayo incident.

"What miffs me," he said, "is that I was getting a blowjob from a beautiful woman, and I stopped so that I could fuck a jar of mayonnaise. That was really stupid."

11 HOW TO MARRY A MILLIONAIRE

MANHATTAN BOASTS A staggering female-to-male ratio: 100 single females to 81 single males. Thanks to these frightful statistics, many city women are forced to settle for jobless men who think a date consists of a forty of Schaefer and a slice of pizza the woman buys for herself. As Lauren Bacall pointed out in *How to Marry a Millionaire*, "Most women use more brains picking a horse in the third at Belmont than they do picking a husband."

Personally, I tend to date the unemployable and insane. My friend Liam once observed that I have the same taste in men as Squeaky Fromme. Having just witnessed my lover fuck a jar of mayonnaise, I agreed.

I needed a little normalcy in my life. I wanted to date a man with a job, someone who could take me out for a meal. I was starting to look consumptive, like a child in an Edward Gorey illustration.

The Learning Annex had been sending me their calendar ever since I took their class on Tolkien. Flipping through it,

I noticed they were offering a class titled "How to Marry Rich" (subtitle: "The Rich Are Going to Marry—Why Not to You?"). I wasn't really looking for a boyfriend, husband, or sugar daddy, but after the Wiggles debacle, trying to meet millionaires seemed like a relatively relaxing concept. I convinced Michael Martin, Nerve's editor in chief, that this would be fascinating fodder for Nerve readers. He wasn't so sure, but acquiesced, seeing as how I'd just narrowly escaped what was probably the Russian Mob.

On the way to class, I ran into my friend Will. "I once slept with a yuppie," he told me. "I felt like a class traitor. She and I both knew it was wrong. It was not unlike sleeping with a crack whore."

The unspoken caste system of New York City dictates that artists and yuppies rarely engage in coitus.

I arrived at class fifteen minutes early. Embarrassed even to be there, I tried to slink past the clerk at the front desk.

"Which class are you here for?" he asked loudly.

"How to marry rich," I whispered.

"Classroom L," he said, pointing to a room in which one dude and several women between the ages of twenty and fifty had begun to assemble. "I'm hoping to get a lot out of this class," the lone dude announced to no one in particular. I sat next to a forty-something redhead in a nurse's uniform. Immediately, I realized I'd made a terrible mistake. Fidgeting excessively and muttering to herself, she removed her shoes and started digging through her purse in a crazed manner.

When all of the seats were filled, our instructor, matchmaker Shoshanna Rikon, strode into the room, clad in a pinstriped mini-suit, the kind Heather Locklear used to wear on *Melrose Place*. "If anyone can't hear me over the air conditioner," announced Shoshanna, "please let me know."

Immediately, the nurse screamed out, "I can't hear you!"

After turning off the A.C., Shoshanna began the lecture. The first order of business was where to find Mr. or Ms. Moneybags. "Location, location, location," she professed. "If there's a line out the door, it's probably a good choice." She suggested hotel bars and well-known spots like the 21 Club, where you can obtain a hamburger for $21. I started to get the feeling that marrying rich was not unlike all other business ventures: you've gotta spend money to make money.

She also suggested pretending to shop in upscale men's clothing stores while secretly browsing for bachelors.

"Where are these places?" the nurse hollered out. "Can you write them down on the chalkboard? You're going too fast. I can't take notes."

Shoshanna distributed a handout that listed various fancy events where one was bound to meet millionaires. "If you can't afford these events, try to get someone to take you, or volunteer for the committee that organizes them." According to Shoshanna, once you finagle your way into one, you will get on mailing lists and make connections for getting invited to future galas. As Shoshanna continued, the nurse interrupted a good ten times to ask nonsensical questions.

"Please save your questions until the end of the class," Shoshanna requested politely.

Insufficiently discouraged, the nurse chimed in again. "If we go to these things, everyone there is gonna know that everyone in this room has no money!"

Having dealt with serial interrupters in the fellatio class,

I knew that if someone didn't quash these outbursts, they would never end.

"Could you please stop interrupting," I said firmly.

"What do you mean?" she asked, taken aback by my boldness.

"Stop interrupting. It's driving everyone here crazy."

"You're a pain in the ass," she shrieked. "Don't sit next to me!"

"Okay, everyone be nice to each other," pleaded Shoshanna. I scooted my chair away from the nurse and looked down at my notebook. I was so nervous about getting attacked after class that I was barely able to take notes. But remarkably, there were no more interruptions.

Moving on to style, Shoshanna suggested we try to emulate the savoir faire of socialites. "First impressions are very important. Men are extremely visual. When it comes to makeup, less is more."

According to research, millionaires don't like fake, chipped, or patterned nails. So if you're looking for a rich hubby, leave the Lee Press-Ons at home. Also according to research—here's another big shocker—millionaires like thin, hot women. Shoshanna recommended we study the pages of *Avenue*, a glossy lifestyle magazine for Manhattan's affluent and socially powerful. She passed a copy around. When it came time for the nurse to pass it to me, she hurled it at me, barely missing my head. Calmly, I collected the magazine and turned its now-crumpled pages. I observed the little black dresses and pointed pumps of the ruling class. My wardrobe of psychedelic micro-minis and colorful platform shoes would apparently not fly in their social circles.

The next order of business was how to find out if your

potential mate is rich—without him or her knowing it. "Look at his shoes," Shoshanna advised, "Or when you're talking, casually flip over his tie and check out the brand." Millionaires, she told us, must engender a certain amount of respect. What they wear is "the uniform they put on when they go to battle to make money."

"Also, get his card and Google him," Shoshanna cautioned. "He might tell you he's a CEO, but he might actually be a CEO for a company that's in the basement of his mother's house."

Once we covered the basics of finding a millionaire, Shoshanna addressed the various methods of getting him "hooked." Among the rules: don't fight with his family, don't call a million times a day, don't waste his time, and don't sleep with him right away. "Let him wine you and dine you," she recommended.

This concept was so foreign to me that I'd actually forgotten the option of being wined and dined existed. Having spent the majority of adulthood surrounded by free-loving artists who can't afford dates, my relationships have always started in bed.

As the class wound to a close, Shoshanna opened the floor to questions. I raised my hand.

"What I don't understand is how do you start talking to a millionaire," I said. "What do I say to strike up a conversation?"

"It's really simple," replied Shoshanna. "All you have to do is say, 'Hello, my name is—'"

"That's it?"

"Yes, and no cheesy pickup lines like, 'Hello my name is blank, do you come here often?'"

"I have a question," piped another student. "If you go on a date with a millionaire, who pays?"

"Never pay," said Shoshanna.

"You don't even do the fake reach for the purse?" the incredulous student asked.

"Nope. You can do something nice for him, but never pay."

"Awesome," the student replied, jotting feverishly in her notebook.

After fielding a few more inquiries, Shoshanna dismissed us. I hightailed it out of there to avoid an after-school throwdown with the nurse.

I called my friend Amy, who agreed to meet me at Brooks Brothers, where we would pretend to shop while covertly trolling for wealthy bachelors. I tied my hair back, slipped on a little black dress, and headed uptown, a modern Holly Golightly in search of a gentleman caller.

As I waited for Amy outside of Brooks Brothers, my eyes were drawn to the window display. It contained mannequins clad in blue trousers emblazoned with little green whales. I'm not so sure I could ever fuck a man who wears such silly pants, I thought. Amy arrived and we ventured inside. Seeing very few bachelors, we wondered how long we could loiter until the salespeople got suspicious. After I drained my girl-lizard in the very clean Brooks Brothers bathroom, we left and headed to Grand Central Station. We'd planned on paying a visit to the Oyster Bar, but noting the lack of elbow room, we opted for the Tropica. Taking a seat at the bar, I noticed that everyone but us had bowls of peanuts. "Maybe only the rich people get peanuts," I ventured.

Next to us, a woman sat doing legal proofreading, effectively cockblocking us from the two attractive men at the end of the bar.

"She needs to save that for the office," Amy said.

"Yeah, you shouldn't proofread while drunk."

"Rich people work too hard."

After imbibing two beverages at the Tropica, we left to seek out greener pastures. We made our way to Beer Bar, which Shoshanna had recommended since it's attached to the MetLife Company. Even though I'm extremely bothered by MetLife's bastardizing of Snoopy in their ad campaigns, I was willing to forgo my principles.

On the Beer Bar's patio, we saw several fetching men clad in suits. We sidled up to the bar, where the bartender handed me what appeared to be a Dixie cup filled with Stella Artois. "Maybe the class should have given us a tutorial on the dine-and-dash technique," I said, noting the inflated price of uptown beer.

A blond girl standing next to me at the bar turned around. Excited that anyone was making contact with me, I perked up. "That's a really cute umbrella," she noted. "But could you please stop stabbing me with it?" As she spoke, I marveled at the fact that her mouth barely moved. I couldn't believe she was producing sound.

"Excuse me," I said, laying my umbrella down. Still, she and her beau moved to the other side of the bar.

Time passed. "I can't believe any of these people have penises or vaginas," I said, observing the crowd.

We sauntered inside and sat down at the bar. Amy struck up a conversation with a nerdy-but-cute Texan who was sipping a gigantic beer. He explained that he was on a break from work and he would have to return shortly.

"I'm really on my last leg," I whispered to Amy. "This is way too exhausting."

Hours had passed, and we'd met only one bachelor. Like most rich people, he worked too much. We finished our drinks and left.

The evening had been a total failure, but no one said it would be easy or quick.

The next morning I called Claudia, who is in a much higher tax bracket than any of my other friends.

"You know all of the rich men are in the Hamptons this weekend," she said.

"I know, but I'm on deadline. There have to be at least a few in town."

We agreed to meet at the Mandarin Oriental bar at eight.

Throwing caution to the wind, I tossed my conservative little black dress aside in favor of my only piece of vintage couture—a pastel Pucci mini-dress given to me by Claudia. I tied my hair back, threw on a pair of pink heels, and pulled out every woman's secret weapon—smoky eyes.

Unfortunately, when we arrived at the Mandarin, we were the only people there. As we sat at the abandoned bar, I confided in Claudia. "I'm terrified of speaking to rich people. I'm used to only talking to crazy artists."

"Wait—you're assuming the rich aren't crazy?"

"Good point."

"Well, this place is dead. Do you want to go somewhere else?"

"Sure."

"Have you ever been to Pastis?" Claudia asked.

"No."

"Oh, we have to go. I'll bet that's where everyone is tonight."

We hailed a cab. "This is like extreme sports," Claudia noted as I twisted my ankle on the cobblestones of Little West Twelfth.

"I know. It should be on ESPN 8: millionaire chasing."

The kindly hostess at Pastis told us that the bar was too crowded and that we'd need to wait five minutes until a few people left. I felt like a small child waiting to go on the Dumbo ride at Disney World. After a few minutes, several drunk people came pouring out and we gained entrance. As we walked toward the bar, a young man leapt in front of me.

"Stop!" he commanded and then took a long look at me. "Beautiful eyes," he concluded. Finally someone noticed! As he moved out of the way, we noticed a dude sporting an eye patch.

"He must be loaded," I proclaimed.

The place was jam-packed with trendy people. Claudia circled the bar like a shark and snagged two seats. All around us, people typed away on their Palm Pilots. A tall blond woman next to me was engaged in a text-message argument with her boyfriend, which she relayed to her friend. "I can't believe he just text-messaged me that!" she cried, staring into her phone.

I eyed a gray-haired gentleman in a navy blazer. "He must be a millionaire," I said.

"No, he's a tourist," Claudia said knowingly. "Okay Rev., before we leave you have to talk to at least one rich guy."

"I'm going to be completely rejected, but you're right." As I spoke, I noticed an attractive young blond man in a pink striped button-down. "Now he's cute," I noted, "and he looks wealthy."

"You have to talk to him. We're not leaving until you do."

I took a deep breath and turned to him. "Hi, I'm Jen," I said, expecting the worst.

"Hi, I'm James," he said, extending a hand.

I turned to Claudia; my eyes bulged in disbelief. She doubled over with laughter.

James and I commenced small talk. I asked him what he did during the day.

"I'm an investment banker," he answered.

I have no idea what investment bankers do. I can only deduce that because the job title includes the word "banker," they must make a lot of money. Because I hadn't read *Forbes* or *The Wall Street Journal* as Shoshanna had suggested, I didn't know how to respond to James. Instead of revealing my ignorance, I quickly changed the subject, telling him I liked his pink shirt. "Mostly only men over sixty-five wear pink," I said. "I always appreciate seeing it on young men."

He in turn complimented the pink highlights in my hair, which I'd done my best to hide.

James bought me a beer and we chatted amorously, our bodies pressed together by the swelling crowd at the bar.

Without going into too many details, I admitted to him that I lived a "very strange" life. This didn't scare him away; instead, he wanted to hear about my various adventures. When I finally looked up from our conversation, I saw that it was one-thirty in the morning. James's friends were leaving for another bar; he invited me along. Remembering Shoshanna's advice to "be a challenge," I told him I needed to go home. Although I failed to obtain the requisite business card, we exchanged digits before saying goodbye.

As I traipsed into my building at 2 AM, past the condom wrappers and the squeaking of giant rats in the walls—who, unlike the rats in *Cinderella*, would never sew me a ball gown—I felt happy to be home. Suddenly my life seemed preferable to the Palm Pilot frenzy I'd just witnessed. What I really wanted was to go downtown and drink forties of Budweiser with people who really knew me. Part of snagging a man means pretending to be perfect until he falls in love with you, whereupon you reveal yourself to be the asshole that you really are. There are few things more satisfying than being with people who know you're a giant asshole, but love you anyway.

After ascending the six urine-scented flights of stairs to my apartment, I passed out, exhausted. Going from bar to bar in search of Mr. Moneybags was physically and emotionally draining. It would have almost been less exhausting to make the millions myself or to visit California and literally mine for gold.

The next day, I wrote the article and figured my gold-digging days were over. Being poor and alone was a lot less work. But as I settled in for a night of Kraft mac'n cheese and tap water, James called.

He wanted to meet for drinks. It hadn't occurred to me that this might happen. Terror struck me as he suggested we meet in my neighborhood, where it's virtually impossible to escape my insane friends. Images of Erin and Orion regaling him with mayonnaise jar–fucking stories danced in my head. I recommended the least popular bar in the neighborhood.

There he bought me a pint and told me about his life. He grew up in Poland, immigrated here, and worked hard for everything he had. He wasn't spoiled or snarky. And he was cute. I forgot that he was of the alien species known as the rich.

Things were going well until he said, "You don't really seem like the kind of girl who hangs out at Pastis."

"I'm not."

"What brought you there?"

Whoever said honesty is the best policy obviously didn't marry a millionaire. I hadn't told James that I was a sex columnist yet. I planned on doing it once he was on his fourth beer. As it turns out, we never made it that far.

He laughed as I told him the various debacles I'd experienced as a sex writer, but I imagine his internal dialogue went something like this: *This girl is fucking nuts and she probably has the clap.*

After a polite second round of drinks, James walked me to my door and kissed me goodnight. He never called again.

12 DUDE FOR A DAY

I'M FAIRLY CONVINCED that I once had a penis, which was chopped off at birth. My predilections for classic rock, domestic beer, and televised sports are really only found among men. I'm also a woman with the morals of a man, or what is commonly referred to as a "slut" in the vernacular. If I didn't have a vagina, I'd probably make a righteous dude.

I found a workshop called "Man for a Day" taught by a drag king performer named Diane Torr. According to her website, she offered women individual makeovers, complete with fake facial hair and instructions on how to behave as men. I contacted Diane, and she agreed to try to make a man out of me.

I wondered if a few lessons and a phony 'stache would be enough to transform me into a believable guy. I'm the size of a diminutive jockey. Short of shooting anabolic steroids into my ass, there's little I can do to change this. The second a woman asked me to open a jar of mayonnaise, my true sex would be revealed.

But I yearned to uncover the secrets of the opposite sex. With the world as my urinal and the wind at my feet, would manhood be one big par-tay? Or would I long for a return to the joys of womanhood? But, most importantly, would chicks dig me?

I told my male friends that I didn't want to half-ass my cross-dressing expedition and therefore needed advice.

"Wait, you're gonna be a man for a day?" my friend John asked. "How will that be different from any other day?"

"Get a jersey with another man's name on it and live vicariously through him," my friend Jeff suggested. "Also, when it comes to talking sports, just look at the front page of ESPN's website. Pretend to be infuriated over whatever is on it. Also, you know the phrase 'the people around the king make the king'? Well, the people around the douchebag make the douchebag. Don't forget that."

I jotted this down.

"Where do I put my stuff?" I asked. The idea of going anywhere sans purse was daunting.

Suggesting that a wallet is a bit too "metro," Bruce advised me to haphazardly stuff everything into my pockets.

As for men's room etiquette: "Shake it more than twice and you're playin' with it," warned my friend Big Mike, adding that no matter how you shake and dance, the last three drops will go down your pants.

It was also recommended I watch *Just One of the Guys*, a film which I happen to own. Although Jeff suggested I watch it for pointers on how not to be a convincing man.

Diane Torr and I exchanged emails, and she encouraged me to start thinking about what kind of man I hoped to be.

Because I am a Leo, I take my hair seriously. I won't cut

it for any reason, not even transvestitism. I would just have to find a masculine guise that entailed long locks. Kat suggested I go for a Yanni look. After all, Yanni managed to get with Linda Evans. But I wanted to find a style I thought was hot. I'm already manlier than most East Village pretty boys, so that look was out. Since I've always been mildly attracted to longhaired stoners, I decided to try for a greasy rock 'n' roll vibe.

For my name, I immediately chose Steve. If I were a dude, my name would undoubtedly be Steve. Big Mike persuaded me to adopt the nickname "Steverino" to clarify that Steve likes to party. Men's men have often commented that I sound like a female Jack Nicholson, so the voice transformation wasn't too difficult. By lowering my voice an octave and emphasizing its crackly undertones, I can easily sound like a man who does fourteen bong hits an hour.

The night before my workshop, I decided to take Steve for a test run with my male buds. In preparation, I picked up a $5 fake mustache and a skull-emblazoned bandanna to conceal my bangs. (A smart move, I thought, considering that the last dudes to wear bangs were probably the Sweet or the Bay City Rollers.) An old pair of jeans, a dirty Black Sabbath T-shirt, aviator glasses, and checkered Vans would complete the look.

At home, I cranked up AC/DC, popped open a tallboy, and commenced my initial makeover, beginning with my breasts. I didn't think it was possible for me to be more flat-chested than I already am. One Ace bandage later, I was proven wrong.

Next, I applied my 'stache using spirit gum and a little eyeliner for shading. Surprisingly, the 'stache served as a sponge, soaking up any Budweiser that managed to escape my gullet. Finally, I slipped out of my dress and into my man clothes. I stared at my duded-up reflection. The man in the mirror appeared to be Derek Smalls from Spinal Tap. I also looked like a narc, the type who might approach you at a party looking for "doobage."

Tom and Mike agreed to meet me at Motor City, a somewhat bad-ass bar where there would surely be a handful of rocker chicks harboring Derek Smalls fantasies. Leaving my apartment, I realized I'd forgotten to wear a "package." Hastily, I grabbed a rolled-up pair of pink knee-highs and stuffed them down my pants.

At the bar, Tom did a double take as I sat next to him. "What's up, Big Guy?" I asked, soliciting a high-five. Soon my second wingman, Mike, joined us. We punched each other good-naturedly and exchanged appropriate manly greetings.

Across the bar, I noticed Jeff, my coworker from the bookstore. I approached him. "How they hangin'?" I inquired. Jeff stared at Steverino, bewildered. "It's me, Jen," I said, waving my hand in front of his face, trying to break the spell.

"Oh my God, you're a dude!" he exclaimed, horrified.

I ordered a Yuengling and rejoined my pals, who regaled me with stories of manliness. "I was at this college bar back in Boston," Tom began. "There were a bunch of students hanging out. Well, all of a sudden this biker gang comes walking in, and the littlest one looked like you. He was the smallest one, so of course he was the meanest. He walked over to the bar where this couple was sitting, and in one motion he pulled the woman's chair out from under her! Her date had no choice but to stand up for his lady's honor, and the tiny biker responded by punching this poor dude in the face from one end of the bar to the next."

A cute blonde sidled up to the bar.

"How you doin'?" I asked her.

"All right." She looked around suspiciously, as if she were afraid Steverino might stain her.

"Are you single?" I asked.

She looked like she'd eaten a bag of Sour Patch candies. "No," she said firmly.

"Okay, your loss, babe," I said as she scurried away as fast as possible. I turned back to the guys. "She was a total lesbian."

"Rev., don't ever ask if they're single," admonished Tom. "Ask them where their boyfriend is."

"Oh," I said. "That way if they have no morals, they can say 'not here.'"

"And those are the girls you want."

"The bartender is hot," gushed Mike.

"Mike," I scolded, "don't work the bartender. Even I know that."

"You just have to do something that sets you apart, and then you can work the bartender."

"Well, I can't. Not after she checked my ID and saw that I'm a woman."

After hoisting a few at the bar and not scoring with any of the laydees, we decided to "make like a tree." We ran into our friend Don, who thought Steverino might have better luck at a party out in Queens. When you are a man you will travel to even the most remote locations in hopes of finding action.

The party in Queens was small and full of people I knew. They all found Steverino "disturbing." My 'stache started to fall off somewhere around my fifth beer. Soon after that, the Ace bandage unfurled; it had loosened from Steve's excessive chest-sweat. When I went to the bathroom, my "package" fell out and barely missed the toilet. The spirit-gum bottle I'd stashed in my pocket for emergency 'stache repairs had leaked and glued my pocket together. Steve had self-destructed. Now I just looked like a dirty woman with stubbly facial hair.

The next morning, I woke up fifteen minutes before my workshop was scheduled to begin. There was no time to shower, which would only make Steve greasier on day two.

Diane met me in the lobby of her building and escorted me into a well-lit dance studio. She began by showing me her portfolio, which was filled with photos of women she'd transformed into men. She then handed me a copy of *FHM* magazine and told me to look for men whose facial hair I wanted to simulate. I found the hottest man in the magazine and said I wanted to look like him. His facial hair was not unlike the ridiculous 'stache I'd donned the night before, only it was paired with a five o'clock shadow and sideburns.

"We can do that," she affirmed.

Realizing I'd forgotten both tighty whities and a fake penis, we walked to a pharmacy in search of penis-making supplies and manties. I was mildly offended when Diane suggested I buy boys' underwear because it might fit better. My manhood had already been insulted, and I wasn't even in costume. I defiantly chose a pair of thirty-two-inch briefs with a gray waistband. We then purchased condoms and cotton balls for stuffing.

Back at the studio, I stuffed as many cotton balls as possible into a condom. "I want to be a little man with a huge penis," I said. I inserted the phallus into my trousers and decided to pack to the left, making sure the bulge was pronounced but not overdone. I practiced penis-shifting in front of the mirror.

"Ooh, your nails are too long. People notice that stuff," Diane said, handing me a pair of clippers. She then pulled out a makeup case filled with fake beard hair in every conceivable color. Taking out two locks of black and brown hair, she began to clip off tiny pieces, which would serve as Steve's scruff. I closed my eyes and almost dozed off as she spirit gummed the hair to my face.

Upon opening my eyes and staring into the mirror, I was amazed at the realism of Diane's facial-hair artistry.

"Wow, you look really scuzzy. That works on you," Diane marveled. "Now you have to figure out Steve's history. Where is he from? What does he do? What turns him on? Does he have any fetishes? Where does he go on vacation? These are all things you need to figure out before we leave."

Somewhere in the furthest corners of my subconscious, I'd known Steve all along. His story came to me quickly. "Steve lives in Jersey City. He has a van and works about once a week as a moving guy. He spends a lot of time smoking weed and hangin' out. He likes big women, reads *Juggs*, but his sexuality is uncomplicated. He claims to have bedded many women, but has only had sex a handful of times. He is constantly in the process of trying to form a band."

"Steve looks a little like a junkie," Diane noted.

"Yeah, but Steve would never admit to being a junkie. He claims he only does heroin socially."

Diane informed me that she was also going to do drag in order to play Steve's buddy. In a matter of minutes she expertly applied her faux facial hair and changed into men's clothes. She looked much cleaner than Steve.

We stood together in front of the mirror.

"We're certainly a couple of dudes," Diane assessed.

She decided that she would be Bob, Steve's uncool friend from the UK, whose main interest lay in talking about ancient civilizations.

"I have a feeling Bob bores Steve to tears," Diane observed.

"Yeah, the only reason he hangs out with Bob is because he thinks Bob might buy him weed. Mostly he just zones out whenever Bob is speaking."

Now that we'd conjured up our characters, it was time for lessons in walking, sitting, gesturing, and making stupid faces. Diane taught me to walk with my feet planted firmly on the ground. "You don't get out of anyone's way," she reinforced. She also taught me to use my thumbs often, to gesture with my fists rather than my fingertips, and never to put my hands on my hips.

After a series of exercises and scene studies between Bob and Steve, we were ready to hit the streets, hoping to find men like Steve whom I could observe and emulate. Our first stop was Washington Square Park. We hung out on a bench, where Bob rambled on about his trip to Cambodia while Steve stared straight ahead obliviously. Finding no Steves in the West Village, we ventured down St. Mark's Place toward Tompkins Square Park.

On St. Mark's, Steverino stopped to flirt with a woman who was giving out smoothie samples and to laugh his ass off at the various novelty T-shirts for sale. "Dude—'Take Me Drunk I'm Home!' I should totally wear that. 'I fucked your boyfriend'—you should wear that, Bob!" At this point, I really started giggling uncontrollably. Steve had fully inhabited my body. I was possessed by a dude. My camaraderie with Bob had grown, too, and he was now laughing along with me. Just a coupla guys bustin' a nut on the corner.

Steve plotted how he was gonna go into the smoothie place and order a bunch of smoothies, drink 'em real fast, and then say, "But, like I thought they were free. The girl outside gave me one for free!" Bob thought this was hilarious.

As we entered the park, politically active young people attempted to hand us leaflets pertaining to the upcoming elections. "I don't vote, dudes," Steve declared, stepping around them.

We sat on a bench and looked for male role models. "There really is no one like you, Steve. You're one of a kind," sighed Bob. Approximately two seconds later, a voice not unlike Steve's boomed out in the distance. "Dude, you totally stole my King Diamond button!" the voice intoned. We turned our heads and observed a shirtless man approaching the perpetrator who allegedly had his King Diamond button.

"Oh my God, that's a total Steve," I gasped.

"Look at his walk," Bob instructed. "He's got a Neanderthal thing going."

"He owns the park."

The two men settled their dispute and left, but soon we saw Steves everywhere. A group of longhaired teenage slackers sunbathed on a blanket. "They're Steves," I noted.

"They're going to be Steves," Bob corrected.

A clean-cut version of Steve passed by. "That hipster is being a Steve in an ironic way," I observed, checking out his perfectly manicured handlebar moustache and Breck Girl hair.

"That girl was checking you out, Steve," Bob said as we passed a young hottie.

"I bet chicks dig Steve because he's so scuzzy."

"And because he doesn't care," Bob added.

"Scha-wing!" I gasped, ogling a girl in a tight Rolling Stones T-shirt who was, believe it or not, smiling at Steve.

I winked at her and she looked away quickly.

Steve tried making eyes at the laydees several times to no avail. I chalked it up to the fact that they simply "couldn't handle" Steve. He was not the kind of man you take home to your family, unless you're trying desperately to rebel against them. Finally, I knew what men meant about wishing women would approach them.

After a heavy dose of girl-watching and jackassery, we decided to head back to the studio due to excessive heat and Steve's declaration that he "totally had to get back to Jersey."

As I slowly let the dude front go, I kind of missed being Steve. He had been the perfect excuse for laziness. I would never just hang out in the park, *but Steve would.* I would never ignore politically active youths handing out leaflets, *but Steve would.* In fact, through Steve I almost achieved a perfect state of "nothingness."

As for whether or not I passed, I made a fairly convincing albeit scuzzy dude. For the most part, people believe what they see on the surface. When I really got into it and started to act the part, *I* almost forgot that beneath it all I had a vulva. In case I'm ever truly famous and need to hide from the paparazzi, or if I'm ever a special agent and need to sneak past armed guards, Steve could serve as the perfect disguise.

And while I didn't make the most Herculean man of all time, I wouldn't hesitate to say that somewhere in the world there's a chick who would dig Steve. I'm not sure I want to meet her, but she's got to be out there.

13 SQUIRTING

ADA WARNED ME not to look at reader comments. "Nerve readers can be kind of mean," she said. And up until the "Dude for a Day" column, I took her advice. Then one night I took a peek.

Most of the comments were complimentary, but a few were so nasty that my fragile ego fell apart. One reader called me "depraved" for having used the men's bathroom dressed as Steverino, while another called my writing "run-of-the-mill porn." Clearly a lot of people hated me.

I went through each article's comments, feeling worse about myself with each passing second.

I called Erin, crying.

"Fuck them," she said, succinctly. "They are just jealous. Did you ever hear the saying, 'People don't want what you have; they just don't want you to have it'? Don't let those sex-hating assholes get to you. You just need to do something more pornographic. I've been thinking: we should try to make you squirt."

Erin always managed to turn the conversation back to either sex or drinking.

"Squirting is all the rage in porn these days," she added.

Squirting by way of a G-spot orgasm had never been at the top of my list of priorities. Maybe it was the name that turned me off: "Grafenberg Spot" is just not that sexy. It sounds like something I slept through in eighth-grade lab science. Even though I'd heard that G-spot orgasms were tremendous, I was happy with my clitoral orgasms. After all, if somethin' ain't broke, don't fix it.

I also wondered if the idea that squirting G-spot orgasms are earth-shattering was part of The Man's plan to make women feel inadequate. One of the great things about being a woman is never clicking on spam emails for products that promise to help you shoot loads across the room.

However, I was not willing to rule it out of my sexual repertoire. A possible bonus: If I were able to find some chemically sensitive paper, I could incorporate squirting into my visual art and revive the action-painting movement.

Though Erin was not a squirter, she'd just stolen a copy of *She Comes First* from the publishing company where she worked. In addition, she sent me a résumé detailing her qualifications as a squirting partner, which consisted of having a tongue and at least ten fingers. Skills and work experience included using toys, not crying during sex, and always paying the rent. Several references were listed, including Janet Reno and the entire roster of the St. Thomas College field hockey team.

In summation, she wrote, "I will not give up till we make you a fountain. I will even take it right in the eye. That is how important this is to me."

Erin and I scheduled our lab for the following week. Because I have a compact vagina and long fingers, I knew where my G-spot was and had petted it many times. But figuring out how to make this petting propel a volcanic reaction would take at least a week's worth of research.

"You've got to do Kegels," my friend Michelle advised.

"Oh, man, I hate working out, even if it's only my vagina," I moaned. I know I should do Kegels every day. I also know I should eat spinach, exercise, and remove my eyeliner before bed, but that doesn't mean I do. Reluctantly, I began doing Kegels—at work, at the bar, on the subway, while watching TV. It was a little like not exercising for ten years and then cramming for a triathlon with only a week to go.

Many of my male friends were eager to discover what techniques could lead to female ejaculation. My friend George Googled squirting and discovered that porn actor and producer Seymore Butts had made a DVD entitled *Seymour Butts' Female Ejaculation: A Complete Guide*. The absurd yet academic title appealed to me. However, I imagined that entering a porn store and requesting such a ridiculous title would be mortifying. To lessen the embarrassment I brought along my friends Amy and Georgia.

Our first stop was sex superstore Babeland, where I didn't find the DVD but did acquire a "Nubby G" vibrator, which is said to stimulate not only the G-spot but the clit and anus as well. According to Babeland employees, this oafish vibrator helped someone they knew ejaculate for the first time. Along with my Nubby G, I picked up a copy of the DVD *How to Female Ejaculate*. According to the cover, it was "the classic—10,000 copies sold!"

From there, we headed up to Times Square, where I

sheepishly wandered into several stores looking for the Seymore Butts video. A porn shop employee named Greg told us they were sold out. "It's definitely one of the best," he added, promising to order it for me.

Later that night, Bruce and I viewed *How to Female Ejaculate*. The DVD opens with host Deborah Sundahl discussing female anatomy. Judging from Deborah's shoulder-padded purple blazer and the Nagel prints behind her, I gathered that the film was shot in the mid-'80s. As for the G-spot, Deborah proclaimed, "If it were any closer, it might bite you!" She then went on to display her own G-spot by turning a speculum on its side.

"It looks like a little snail," I marveled.

Soon, a trio of Deborah's squirter friends joined her.

"Look, two of them are wearing hats," Bruce observed. "Maybe that has something to do with it."

The squirters proceeded to discuss their first ejaculation experiences and the consistency of their ejaculate—what it felt, smelled, and even tasted like.

"Let's get to the squirting!" I cried.

"It's made by women, so of course they have to talk about it a lot before they do it," Bruce noted.

We were forced to eat our condescending words when the women suddenly began to squirt. Bruce literally jumped out of his seat as a lanky brunette in crotchless Calvin Klein panties, suspenders, and requisite hat shot enough clear fluid to drown a small mammal.

"That's amazing! How cool would it be to jizz on a man's face?" I pronounced, inspired.

The following day, I picked up my Seymore Butts video, popped it in the DVD player, and awaited instruction, Nubby

G in hand and Astroglide at my side. Unlike most male adult stars, Seymore Butts has high cheekbones and a cute smile. He is a male porn star who might actually turn women on.

The film began with Seymore standing in the rain getting drenched, then shaking out his lovely ringlets and promising to teach viewers everything they wanted to know about female ejaculation. His sermon was interrupted by a phone call from his mother, which he went inside to answer.

From then on, the Butts residence was awash in activity. It was like he was a latter-day Mr. Rogers; his telephone and doorbell were constantly ringing. Only, in this land of make-believe, it wasn't Mr. McFeely at the door but Tina, a blonde with basketball boobs who wound up engaging in coitus with another visitor to the Butts home. In one scene, a pants-less brunette strolled through Seymour's living room to retrieve her trousers from the laundry room. Shockingly, she never made it to the laundry room but instead lost her top, her bra, and about a half-gallon of she-jizz.

Amid the unbelievable scenarios, viewers were treated to tips on squirting. Tina demonstrated advanced and beginner Kegels, and Seymore boxed a plastic "Tae Bo buddy" while explaining that wrist and forearm strength are crucial to eliciting female ejaculations from your partner.

Female Ejaculation: A Complete Guide is one of the loudest pornographic videos I've ever viewed. Inordinate amounts of wailing and moaning accompanied each squirting episode. After viewing the first two hours of footage, I wandered into my kitchen and realized my new next-door neighbors were having a fancy rooftop cocktail party while all my windows were wide open. I'm lucky no one called the cops.

Horrified, I ventured back inside my bedroom, turned

down the volume, and decided to do a little exploring. Splaying my legs, I fiddled with my G-spot, making a come-hither motion with my fingers. I draped a condom over the Nubby G and coated it with lube. Evidently my eyes had been bigger than my vagina when I purchased the Nubby: its fat, curved head barely fit. When I finally managed to insert it, the pressure was too much for my clit. Within a minute or two, I achieved a satisfying clitoral orgasm that made me wonder why exactly I was bothering with the G-spot.

If I were going to have a full-on G-spot orgasm, I would have to keep my fingers away from my clit, a feat that would possibly require restraints. Placing the Nubby G far out of reach, I tried again, this time using my fingers and the rapid motions I'd witnessed Seymore use. I clenched my PC muscles, sweated and strained, but produced no fountain.

Frustrated, I called Faceboy. Knowing he had experience with squirters, I thought he could give me advice.

"Face, I've been rubbing my G-spot for an hour," I said. "I feel like I'm ready to squirt but can't."

"Well, what kind of sensations are you having?" he asked.

"I feel the G-spot swell up and get hard. And it feels like I have to pee."

"You know how when you pee, you just let go? That's what you have to do, just let go."

"What if I pee?"

"You won't. But if you're really worried, try not drinking beer beforehand."

"Sexual activity without beer—that's probably not going to happen. Also, I have to pee all the time anyway. I go through 90 percent of my life having to pee, and the other 10 percent looking for places to pee."

I live in constant fear of pissing myself due to my pea-sized bladder, but Faceboy was right. I would have to get over my phobia of pissing the bed before I could produce the glorious geysers I'd witnessed onscreen.

"Erin, I'm worried I might pee on you," I told my lab partner when she arrived at my apartment carrying her hot copy of *She Comes First*.

"I really wouldn't care," she assured me. "And I've been doing serious research. You're not gonna pee on me. We're gonna make this happen."

"It could take a long time."

"If it takes all night."

Like a junior scientist who had just discovered the explosive qualities of baking soda and vinegar, Erin excitedly shared her findings. Opening the pages of *She Comes First*, she pointed to a line drawing of the urethral sponge and began explaining what happens when it fills with ejaculate.

"What are those squiggly lines?" I asked, confused by the abstract expressionist nature of the image.

"I think those are supposed to be pubes."

"Why did they have to draw in the pubes?"

"Because that's the mons pubis."

"Yeah, but still it seems a little detail oriented."

"Maybe the guy just digs pubes."

Erin put the book down and we went into my boudoir, where I put on *How to Female Ejaculate* and fast-forwarded to the ejaculations.

"You know, they really don't tell you exactly how to do it in this video," Erin said.

"I know. It's like they're showing off."

Realizing Erin was bored, I put on the more modern Seymore Butts DVD.

"I'm really intimidated," I said, watching the fountains of clear liquid pouring forth from the actresses onscreen.

"Don't be intimidated. They're in porn because they can do that. They're experts. That's why they get paid the big bucks."

"I don't think I can do it."

"You can do it. Turn that off and get naked."

I stripped and lay some towels down on the bed, thrilled that, like my male counterparts, I now had a jizz rag.

"Do you want to get naked, too?" I asked Erin, who still wore jeans and a T-shirt.

"No. This is all about you. I'm just here to facilitate. It does feel a little technical, though."

"Yeah, it's like we're about to do surgery."

Some mood lighting and incense remedied the situation. I repositioned myself on the bed and Erin poured a heavy coat of lube over my pudenda. Slowly she spread the lube around and inserted a finger. Luckily she had short nails.

"Do you feel my G-spot?" I asked, excitedly. "It feels like a rough sponge, almost like a loofah."

"Hold on. We're not there yet," she said, teasing me with her fingers and tongue until lube became superfluous.

She slid two fingers inside me, making the sign of Satan as she began to apply pressure to my G-Spot. She worked her fingers in and out, softly at first, and then hard and fast.

Noises escaped my mouth not unlike those of a seal. It must've looked and sounded like Erin was beating the shit out of me, because JJ darted into the bedroom and started going nuts.

"I can't squirt with this commotion," I sighed, rising from the bed and relegating JJ to the kitchen, where she shivered dramatically.

"Okay, back to work," I stated, reclining back on the bed, my G-spot still swollen and aching for relief.

Erin reinserted her fingers, rolling them over the ridges of my sweet spot and settling into a repetitive motion whereby she pressed down on the G. Minutes passed, and with each minute my apparent urge to pee grew stronger. My PC muscles contracted around her fingers, but she wouldn't stop.

"Oh my God, it's killing me!" I screamed. "Please stop!"

"Really?"

"No!"

I begged her to stop several times and then begged her to keep going several times, all while grunting, moaning, and sweating. I tried to "let go," as I'd been instructed to do, but nothing happened. I pressed down like I was draining my kitty and nothing happened. Erin's face was inches from my crotch. She wore a look of pained determination. If you remember the scene in *Alien* where John Hurt's stomach bursts open and he gives birth to alien spawn, you'll have some idea of what my face looked like.

Usually when I build up to orgasm I'm entertaining dirty thoughts, but I was entertaining no thoughts whatsoever. I was just focusing on the intense, unusual sensation in my crotch. I tried to sit up to lessen the pressure.

"No, lie back down!" Erin commanded.

I lay back down and lifted my legs up, in what must've been a really unflattering move.

And then, much to my surprise, I squirted. The feeling

that I had to pee was gone, yet I hadn't peed; I had come instead! I stared down at my vagina, amazed.

"Oh my God! You did it!" Erin screamed.

We hugged and rolled around on the bed together like we'd just won the lottery. As we collected ourselves, I immediately began asking questions regarding the aesthetic of my squirt. Because we weren't underwater, I knew it hadn't been as impressive as the ejaculations I'd watched onscreen. Still, I was a little disappointed when Erin referred to my ejaculation as "cute."

"It sprayed out about four inches. It was like a little fountain," she informed me.

"Did it get in your hair?" I asked.

"No. It didn't get that far."

Disappointed by my lack of distance and aim, we tried a few times to elicit another ejaculation, to no avail. I even convinced Erin to get naked and allow me to dip my hands in her honey pot.

Unable to muster further ejaculations, we gave up and went to a nearby bar, where we discussed our G-spots ad nauseam.

What fascinates me most about the G-spot is how big it gets when aroused, like a sponge that expands when it fills with liquid. I know it's not a sexy adjective, but the G-spot is really neat.

And I was proud of my come shot. I spent the following day boasting to friends that I'd squirted.

"Was it fun?" Tom asked.

"It was fun, but it was a lot of pressure. I didn't want to disappoint."

"Now you know how we feel," he said.

29 I'LL NEVER WASH THIS VAGINA AGAIN

THE LOWER EAST Side is a small town, one that's full of slutty bisexual people who've all slept with each other. It had become impossible for me to leave my apartment without running into someone I'd seen naked. Nick, in particular, showed up everywhere I went. Even though I told him we were through, he believed he could win me back. I catered to this delusion by continuing to sleep with him occasionally. I was lonely and he was a good lover. And a good lover, no matter how cruel, is hard to give up. I needed rehab for my addiction to Nick's penis.

I had to regain my fabulosity, sanity, and freedom, which meant getting as far away from the Lower East Side as possible.

The Trachtenburg Slide Show Family Players invited me to be their opening act during a run at London's Soho Theatre, and I jumped at the chance. The Slide Show Players were the new millennium's answer to the Partridge Family. Jason Trachtenburg (the dad) played keyboards and sang. Tina Piña Trachtenburg (the mom) operated the slide projector and designed their matching costumes. And Rachel Piña Trachtenburg (the daughter), an adorable pre-teen, played the drums. Jason composed songs based on slide collections they found at flea markets. Their act had grown so popular they were the first unsigned band to play on *Late Night with Conan O'Brien*.

I'd already toured America with them in 2003 and had been well received in places like Iowa and Michigan. Tina said, "The great thing about you opening for us is that by comparison, we don't seem so weird."

The only bad thing about going to London was that I couldn't bring JJ. Faceboy agreed to watch her while I sought refuge, fame, and fortune across the Atlantic.

On my second day in London, Rachel came bounding out of our dressing room, holding a bag.

"Look! Someone got you a present!" she announced.

Everyone gathered around to see what was inside. Opening the bag, I discovered a 4-pack of Budweiser, a box of chocolates, and a letter from a commissioning editor at one of the biggest publishing houses in the UK. "I'd be very interested in the possibility of you writing a book for us," the letter stated.

The editor had bought a copy of my first book, *Reverend Jen's Really Cool Neighborhood* after my performance and deemed it "hilarious." I'd been overseas for two days and had already gotten more attention from publishers than I had in fifteen years of living in New York. Like the Beatles, I'd been forced to leave my own country to find success.

On my first night off from performing, I met up with a London-based band that had played at my open mike a few months earlier. They'd given me one of their homemade CDs, which had since replaced Led Zeppelin in my "most listened to" category. When I'd emailed the lead singer, Malcolm, to let him know I was coming, he'd promised to take me on a "proper English date." This, I learned, meant sneaking into his show by pretending to be in the band, imbibing obscene amounts of beer on an empty stomach, raising hell in a post-show bar-hopping frenzy, receiving a lesson in Cockney rhyming slang, and getting thrown off the tube at 12:30 AM. Malcolm and his friends made my friends in New York seem like teetotaling members of a Christian youth group.

Having been booted from the tube, we wandered outside, where it began to pour. As we stood in the middle of Piccadilly Circus, drunk, confused, and wet, Malcolm kissed me. And it did not matter that my hair was ruined or that my false eyelashes were falling off because I was kissing my fave rock star. I felt like Marcia Brady when she got with Davy Jones and announced that she would never wash the hand he'd kissed again. Except Malcolm kissed a lot more than my hand that night.

I awoke feeling like I needed an IV drip. Malcolm, on the other hand, was fine and announced he was off to a recording session with "A&R geezers." I realized that if I stayed out with him every night, I'd need Betty Ford upon my return.

So I divided my time between running around with Malcolm and performing and hanging out with Jason, Tina, and Rachel. Jason was convinced I needed to date a *silver fox*: someone older, distinguished, wealthy, and simply grooving with the eternal now. Specifically, he thought I should date Barry Gibb, but if he wasn't available, Jason thought any silver fox would do.

The previous year a silver fox who claimed to have written "All Out of Love" for Air Supply had invited Jason to a private drinking club called Blacks. Jason had since been made an honorary member there and could bring me with him when he went. The fact that I'm American, and an American writer at that, made me exotic in London. (This is probably why Henry Miller got so much ass in Europe.) My strange voice, which has been described as "Tom Waits meets Dakota Fanning," was deemed adorable by the men at Blacks, who called me "love," bought me drinks, and told me I was pretty. Soon I was declared an honorary member of Blacks as well.

Blacks was crawling with silver foxes, gorgeous older men who had survived the '70s but hadn't bothered with rehab.

One night there, I noticed the sexiest longhaired silver fox I'd ever seen. He was staring at me and smiling, the tired smile of someone who'd done copious amounts of drugs. He looked like a weathered rock star.

"You're an elf," he said, noticing my ears. "Come talk with me." His voice made it even more obvious than his appearance that he'd lived a crazy life. He sounded like Keith Richards, only more exhausted.

His name was Anthony.

"I really want to kiss you," he said two minutes into our conversation.

"I don't think that's such a good idea," I told him, not wanting to appear to be a drunken whore in front of the clientele of Blacks. Despite this, he leaned over and kissed me.

Anthony told me he had a house in Spain, which he'd just returned from with his girlfriend. He'd broken up with her upon his return, when he realized he could no longer stand her. Because I was getting drunk quickly, the conversation is a blur. But I do remember that several sentences were punctuated with Anthony sticking his tongue down my throat.

On our first date a few nights later, I tried to find out where the hell Anthony came from. It appeared his sole occupation was hangin' out. Since most of his stories were about Quaaludes and blowjobs, his origins remain a mystery to this day. I don't know if Anthony even knew where he came from or what he did.

"So the last time I was in America, I was basically kidnapped by these two women, and they, like, slipped me a Quaalude, and the next thing I know, I wake up on a beach in Florida and one of them is giving me a blowjob. It would have been better if they hadn't been so rough looking."

I listened, enraptured.

"Acid in the '70s was *really* strong. I can never do it again," he said.

"I should probably stay away from it, too."

He kissed me.

"You are a naughty elf. I can't wait to take you home and lick your pussy," he whispered, slipping his hand under my mini-dress. We'd been out together for ten minutes. Because British men like drinking as much as they like sex, it was a while before he got to my pussy. He first took me to a tiny drinking club filled with about a dozen aristocratic lunatics who were drinking themselves to death. Upon entering the club, a woman named Angie, who happened to be one of Anthony's ex-girlfriends, screamed at me indecipherably about dildos. Shortly thereafter, a one-armed man in a suit called me a "fucking fascist" upon discovering I was American.

"Don't call Jen a fascist," Anthony said, defending my honor. "She's a groovy girl."

"Fascist!" he screamed.

"Get lost, you bastard!" Anthony screamed.

The one-armed man walked away and came back with a round of drinks.

"Is everyone here insane?" I asked.

"No, they're all just alcoholics except for Angie. She's insane and then she became a crackhead and that made it worse. I'll never forget this one story she told me about rehab," Anthony continued. "Every day the patients would get together and discuss their experiences of the day before. Well this one crackhead got up and said, 'I had a horrible nightmare last night. I was in a hot tub with Angie, and we were both naked, and she was *hogging the crackpipe!*'"

"That really says it all about crack."

For hours Anthony regaled me with similar stories until he finally took me home and fulfilled his earlier promise. I, in turn, performed several goodwill ambassadorial duties.

I liked both Anthony and Malcolm more than any of the men I'd recently been out with in New York. They had manners, charm, and accents that made my G-spot spontaneously combust. Plus I figured men who lived thousands of miles away from me couldn't ruin my life. If things went south with them, they wouldn't ride their skateboards back and forth in front of the bookstore where I worked all day long or stalk me at my open mike.

I'd never met anyone remotely like Anthony. He had fallen off the space-time continuum. He called me "priestess," gave me backrubs, and made me tea in the morning. Though I live in a psychedelic troll museum, his apartment was even stranger. The entire loft was covered in murals and hieroglyphics. In his bedroom, he'd painted random words all over the walls.

"What's up with all the words?" I asked.

"Well, you see, I kept seeing things in the walls like faces and bodies and trees. You wouldn't believe how many faces are in these walls, so I painted the words as a distraction. Plus I like the way cats purr," he noted, pointing to the word "purr" above his door.

I was starting to realize that no matter how much I liked Anthony, he was so spent he would probably never make it through customs.

Jason agreed. "Can you imagine that guy at an airport? He'd be so confused."

Anthony was something none of the "angry young men" I'd dated in New York ever were: he was a mystery. I was so used to New Yorkers telling me everything about themselves within the first five minutes of meeting them that I'd forgotten what it was like to be intrigued by someone. It was life-affirming to meet someone who actually didn't have a blog or MySpace account. I wanted to spend a lifetime listening to Anthony's stories. Sadly, I only had a few days. My time in England was running out, and I knew that he belonged to London's Soho as much as I belonged to the Lower East Side.

On my last night there, I went to see Malcolm's band play, then ran to the theater for a performance of my own. Anthony was in the front row, and he giggled throughout my entire set as if he was having an acid flashback.

In the dressing room, I told Tina where Anthony had been sitting.

"Him? He's like a rock star! I was so intimidated."

"But he's not a rock star," I mused. "He's more like an art star."

On my way to the greenroom, the stage manager handed

me a note, explaining, "This is from a friend of yours who was really drunk."

Sorry I didn't say a proper goodbye. Malcom.

I'd been in London less than three weeks, and my love life was already becoming complicated.

Peeking outside, I saw Anthony waiting for me.

He led me down a cobblestone street to a tiny bar that evoked a Charles Dickens novel.

"This bar used to be owned by a friend of mine," he explained, "who drank herself to death. She'd gone to the doctor, and he said, 'If you have another drink, you will die.' The next day she had a drink and she died, but at least she died doing what she loved."

"I'm gonna miss you," I said.

"I wish you could stay here with me, but I know you love that little dog more than anything."

"Maybe I can sneak her on a boat or something."

We made one last stop at Blacks before heading back to Anthony's loft.

As I fell asleep curled up in his arms, he murmured, "You're a beautiful girl, Jen."

And for the first time in years, I really felt like one.

15 PRINCESS REFORM SCHOOL

THOUGH I MISSED swinging London, there was no time to wax nostalgic. I'd been cast in an independent feature film that was set to shoot a few days after my return. I'd auditioned on a lark, not realizing they might cast someone whose acting experience consisted solely of appearances on wacky cable access shows.

Now I was going to have to wake up at 5 AM every day for two weeks to play "Jessica," a soulless yuppie who cheats on her husband.

The publishers in London, who'd left a gift of beer in my dressing room, were also hankering to read my book, a memoir. They'd taken me out to lunch and suggested I write such a book, only to find I'd already begun one. Though I was only thirty-three, I'd already developed the necessary delusions of grandeur to start writing my life story.

And my column was due. As usual, I had no idea what to write about.

Consulting my Rolodex of freaks, I came across a character I'd almost forgotten: the Headmaster.

I'd first met the Headmaster at one of Abby Ehmann's "sexy soirees" the previous winter. Abby had interviewed me years ago for her magazine *Extreme Fetish,* and we'd since become friends. The *New York Press* voted her soirees "best orgies," but after attending one, I found they were more like a cross between an orgy and a backyard barbeque. If partygoers wanted to get naked and lick testicles, they could. If they simply wanted to eat pretzels, watch porn, and make chitchat, they could do that, too. The soirees were also BYOB; hence they were popular among impoverished artists who refused to let a lack of funds prevent them from engaging in sex with multiple partners.

I made the mistake of smoking pot at my first sexy soiree; it's a drug that really has no place at an orgy. I spent the next several hours feeling paranoid when I should have been feeling uninhibited. Hence I learned my first rule of orgy enjoyment: stick to wine like the Romans did (or even Budweiser).

As I gnawed on pretzel knots and stared at a couple doing it next to me, the Headmaster introduced himself. He had old-fashioned movie-star good looks and he professed to run a "Princess Reform School," an S&M academy devoted to demonstrating the joy of submission to prima donnas. He knew who I was from the performance scene and seemed to think I was just such a creature. He gave me his card.

He then led me into a private room, stripped me bare, and worked a vibrator against my kitty until I came.

The following week, I used his card. He asked me to meet him at a Barnes & Noble on the Upper West Side, wearing my coat and nothing else. It being winter, he also afforded me the luxury of thigh-high tights and boots.

Narrowly avoiding vaginal frostbite, I made it to Barnes & Noble, where he proposed we head to a nearby watering hole.

"Can I take your coat?" he asked. Absentmindedly, I almost handed it to him. As we chatted I realized that, odd as the Headmaster's sexual proclivities were, he was way too normal for me. He worked for a newspaper and lived uptown, far from the chaos of the art star scene.

Our chatter soon ended as the Headmaster pulled his barstool close enough to mine that he was able to thrust a bullet vibrator under my coat and between my legs without anyone else noticing. As perfectly normal businesspeople sipped their Pinot Grigio and Shiraz all around me, I came to the brink of a screaming orgasm.

All this before my sex column even premiered.

It appeared it was time to use the Headmaster's card again.

"I'd like to enroll in the PRS," I told him.

"Well, young lady, you're going to have to fill out our online enrollment."

The application process for Princess Reform School was so complex it would put Harvard's to shame. Fortunately, unlike Harvard, one can obtain admittance simply by completing an online questionnaire, which is designed to determine whether you are a "tragic beauty" in need of humility. Because the Headmaster had already deemed me enough of a princess to qualify for admission, I sent him an email requesting a scholarship, since I'd be writing about the process. The Headmaster agreed to give me a full scholarship but insisted I would have to "work hard for it."

Unlike other reform schools, which are devoted to making bad students good, Princess Reform School is dedicated to making good students bad. The Headmaster started the school several years ago to minister to the needs of a frustrated ex-model, but now he accepts anyone who is "too gorgeous for her own good." A further perusal of the PRS web site revealed that the school dress code forbade panties, hemlines lower than mid-thigh, and heels shorter than three inches. The curriculum page listed dirty talk, bisexual exploration, bondage, and sensual submission. It was also noted that the Headmaster devised an individualized curriculum for each student according to her needs, level of experience, and aspirations.

For my first lesson, the Headmaster suggested he do an "outcall." I was to be homeschooled. He asked me to list and rank my "problem areas." Was I too modest, too bratty, or too haughty? Perhaps I was insufficiently skilled in erotic service? Although I'd gotten naked for about half of my columns, I was still a shrinking violet when it came to public nudity, so I ranked modesty high. "Shyness while engaging in dirty talk," "sexual laziness," and "a general insolence toward authority" also made the list.

The reformatory-princess uniform varied, depending on the assignment. The Headmaster insisted I wear a classic schoolgirl outfit. Luckily, I already owned everything but a white shirt, which I easily obtained at a back-to-school sale around the corner.

The Headmaster arrived for my tutorial jauntily carrying a riding crop and a bag of "school supplies."

We proceeded into my boudoir, where we began with a remedial kneeling lesson. Kneeling might seem like an obvious skill, but there are subcategories which reformatory princesses are required to master. The first position involves simply going down on one's knees. "Arch," on the other hand, entails both kneeling and leaning back toward the floor.

"I think I did this in my *David Carradine's Kung Fu Workout* video," I said, straining to curve my back like a yogi.

"Submissive position!" the Headmaster commanded. I obeyed, thrusting my buttocks toward the heavens, whereupon they were greeted with a hard spanking. Luckily my ass is the fattest part of my body, enabling me to take a spanking that would reduce a lesser pupil to tears. When my amazing threshold for ass pain became apparent, the Headmaster moved on to the riding crop.

After learning to kneel, I learned the "display position," which is performed by standing up with your hands behind your head. Once I was in place, the Headmaster unbuckled my mini-kilt, revealing my vulva. As I stood bare-assed before the Headmaster, he produced a soft blindfold, which he wrapped around my head. From years of cheating during piñata demolitions, I knew that most blindfolds aren't effective. But the Headmaster's blindfold completely blinded me. It was disorienting and frustrating. But as he slowly unbuttoned my shirt and caressed my chest, I became aroused. "You can leave your tie on," he conceded.

"Thank goodness. I was worried I'd have to be naked."

Once I was disrobed (with the exception of knee socks and tie), the Headmaster assailed my torso with the riding crop. However, he managed to strike a balance between pain and pleasure, stroking my weary body lovingly in between punishments. He placed furry handcuffs on my wrists, then clasped them together behind my back, immobilizing my hands should I want to touch myself. And I certainly did want to touch myself. However, a princess must learn to give pleasure before she can receive it, and I was soon back on my knees, delivering an exemplary oral report.

The Headmaster removed my cuffs and treated me to tickle torture with giant pink feathers. I writhed and wiggled as he teased my clit with his fingers. Despite my arousal, the Headmaster informed me that I wouldn't be allowed to orgasm until graduation.

"How soon can I graduate?" I asked.

My professor then informed me of an upcoming sexy soiree. I would be permitted to graduate if I attended and underwent various rites of public chastisement and nudity. The thought filled me with dread. I immediately visualized *The Story of O,* and the scene in which O is forced to attend a party wearing an owl mask and nothing else. This panicked me. Not only that, there would certainly be people I knew at the soiree. I manage to embarrass myself enough at parties while clothed. Who knew what kind of gossip I would inspire when naked? Moreover, I'm so vain that I put on lip gloss to go to Kinko's. The idea of others witnessing my pasty ass jiggle in public freaked me out.

But if I were to overcome my princess pride, I would have to face and conquer my fears. I agreed to attend the party on the condition that I would be treated to a favorable commencement ceremony involving earth-shattering orgasms. The Headmaster assented, then assigned homework: I was to go out in public wearing a mini-skirt with no panties.

Naturally, the next day was one of the windiest days of the year. As I crossed Delancey Street, a gale-force wind whipped my skirt up. I shocked an entire double-decker bus full of tourists by inadvertently exposing my hairless clam.

To save time, I multitasked by not wearing panties to Barnes & Noble, where I hoped to peruse a copy of *Erotic Surrender: The Sensual Joys of Female Submission.* (It's recommended reading for reformatory princesses.) After locating the book, I slid onto a wooden chair and prayed a splinter wouldn't pierce my labia. I tried to concentrate, but being pantyless is a lot like being stoned: you think everyone knows. I'd glance at a page and then nervously around the bookstore. Soon I gave up. Luckily, I have a lot of experience bullshitting my way to graduation.

On graduation night, I was more nervous than I'd been at college commencement.

For moral support, I invited my friend Amy, who'd shopped for instructional squirting videos with me a few months earlier, and another friend, Natalie. They agreed not to look if I did anything too embarrassing. We got to the party shortly after midnight. Inside, I found the Headmaster lounging in a faux-fur-pillow–laden room full of hot people and a smattering of awkward dudes.

After I nervously downed two cans of Budweiser, the Headmaster suggested we get started. He motioned me over to a large wooden X that was bolted to the wall, the type that might have been used in a religious inquisition of yester-year. The same blindfold he'd used in my previous lesson was affixed over my eyes, preventing me from making any visual observations throughout the next portion of the lab. Amy and Natalie giggled in the background.

The Headmaster gently took my wrists and lifted them over my head, spreading them out in a jumping-jack position. Then, he shackled them to the X. *I guess there's nothing I can do about it now*, I thought. I briefly wished I had another Budweiser and considered asking Amy or Natalie to feed me one, since I couldn't use my hands. But I decided that requesting anything would be far too haughty. I was literally in no position to make demands.

Once I got over my desire for beer, being shackled was

actually sort of relaxing. The best thing about being tied up is that you don't have to do any work.

The Headmaster proceeded to spank, flog, and paddle me. I yelped as if I'd just jumped into an ice-cold swimming pool, dancing a veritable jig away from the implements of anguish. In the background, people conversed casually, as if I weren't being tortured only a few feet away.

The Headmaster unfastened my wrist cuffs. "Am I done?" I asked.

"You have a long way to go, young lady," he growled, removing my shirt and refastening the cuffs over my head. He grabbed my ankles, separated them, and shackled them to the base of the X. Then he walked away.

"Where are you going?" I asked fearfully as his footsteps faded into the distance. "How long am I gonna be here?" I grew seriously concerned that I'd have to stay up there all night while everyone else had fun.

Partygoers came and went, occasionally commenting on my bound, half-naked presence. Across the room, the Headmaster discussed varieties of vibrators with my friends. Every so often someone spanked, paddled, or touched me.

After what seemed like several hours, the Headmaster returned, unfastened my skirt, and let it drop. To my horror, I was naked—again, except for my tie and knee socks—in a room full of people. Luckily, I couldn't see them.

The sound of the Headmaster firing up a high-powered vibrator delighted my ears. He ran the device up and down the insides of my thighs. My flesh quivered and I managed to utter, "Thank you, sir." My gratitude was rewarded as the vibrator was thrust between my legs. A hoop with long feathers attached to the sides was then draped around my body, encasing me in plumage. The feathers, combined with the restraints and vibrator, drove me out of my head. The vibrator seemed to be set on a speed equivalent to that of a Black & Decker power sander. And unless the Headmaster had transformed into Doctor Octopus while I was blindfolded, others must have helped him wield the array of sensory devices that graced my skin, converging to give me three extremely un-princess-like orgasms.

I can only imagine how asinine I must have looked: convulsing in orgasm, covered in feathers, tied up with a vibrator pressed to my clit, wearing nothing but a tie and socks. It sort of makes wearing a lampshade on your head at the office holiday party seem acceptable.

I hung from my shackles like a prisoner at a Renaissance Fair, reluctant to move or function. I simply wanted to sway from my shackles, soaking up the total relaxation that follows such monumental decadence. Unfortunately, other partygoers were upset that I was hogging the X. They asked the Headmaster to remove me so they could have their asses whipped, too.

He freed my limbs and removed my blindfold.

"Congratulations, Princess Jen. You've graduated. I think you might even qualify for a teaching assistantship," the Headmaster said proudly.

My friend Ken appeared carrying a pitcher of absinthe. He poured several rounds for everyone until we were all slightly out of our heads.

The Headmaster suggested we "have some fun" and led me to an adjoining room where about ten naked people were sprawled out on a giant bed, fucking.

This was *not* part of the experiment. But when in Rome . . .

I dove into the sea of bodies, as did the Headmaster. A woman climbed on top of him and fellated him as I looked on, while another woman climbed between my legs and licked my pussy while random hands groped me.

Though I felt quite popular, I wasn't sure I wanted to come into contact with unknown dick. I rolled on top of a woman and began giving her head. Looking up I smiled at the Headmaster, who smiled back.

It felt nice and soft though strangely asexual. It was like one big pajama jammy jam where everyone forgot their pajamas. I almost felt like taking a nap. Only in retrospect was it jackable.

Ken opened the door slightly and I saw Amy peek her head in. It was my cue to leave. I blew the professor a kiss and tiptoed out the door.

"How long was I dangling from that X?" I asked Amy as we left the party.

"I don't know. It seemed like an hour, maybe an hour and a half."

"No! Really? I couldn't tell. It's not like I could look at a watch."

"You would've been up there longer except that girl kicked you off. You were getting all of the attention. I don't think she liked that."

"I was hogging the X. It was really unfair."

According to the Headmaster, I'd been an ideal student. (He didn't know I skipped the recommended reading!)

Maybe it's because I'm not as haughty and insolent as I thought. But more likely the reason is that I found my tutor sexy. With a hot enough teacher, *any subject* can be interesting. I'd study advanced calculus if a shirtless Legolas taught it.

Aside from that, I embraced the chance to relinquish my power temporarily. When I stepped away from my shackles, it was not without sadness. Being tied up and blindfolded freed me from the world of normal human interaction. It was like being a work of art that partygoers could stare at and even touch. Yet I'd been unable to stare or touch back. Surprisingly, I hadn't felt powerless or ashamed as I'd expected. I felt appreciated and beautiful, if only on the most superficial level.

I fully understood why O allowed her lover to take her to a party in a crazy owl mask and nothing else: because it's the ultimate narcissistic high.

16 BABY TALK

ABOUT A WEEK into making the movie, I discovered something about acting: I hate it. You wake up early, sit around all day, and then recite someone else's script. This is why so many actors go insane.

To liven things up, I started fucking one of my costars—not the actor playing my husband or the actor playing my lover, but the actor playing the private detective hired by my husband to follow my lover and me around. The affair lasted two days until his scenes were shot and he went back to Canada where he lived.

This left me free to spend the remainder of my time on the set penning letters to Anthony. We'd promised to keep in touch, and it was a promise I intended to keep. Nick was still appearing at my open mike every week and calling me practically every day, but I told him I'd fallen for someone in England. After being treated like a goddess overseas, there was no way I would go back to letting some American dude treat me like crap.

The shoot ended and my next column was due a few days later.

My friends Jen and Hank, who'd met on the set of my play, *Lord of the Cockrings*, had recently given birth to an adorable baby boy named Henry. Jen, who was a fan of my column, suggested motherhood as an experiment.

"After all, it's the result of sex," she said.

The Princess Reform School piece had been so dirty I liked the idea of doing something G-rated. I imagined some dude who'd jacked to the reform school piece anxiously awaiting my next story, only to find it full of dirty diapers and baby food. Something in me delighted in making readers flaccid.

And motherhood wasn't far from my mind. Not that my biological clock was ticking—I'd never had the instinct to breed. But plenty of my friends were starting to have babies. My sister, who was only two years older than me, already had two kids. When her first son was born, I even tried to help out in the delivery room. Despite my best efforts, I did little but stare in horror as the doctor used what looked like a Flowbee to suck the newborn's head out of my sister's vag.

Since then I'd been relegated to the position of wacky aunt, which is the polite term for a thirty-three-year-old woman who still sits at the children's table during family functions. In all, I had six nieces and nephews, but still had never changed a diaper or prepared a bottle. The great thing about being a wacky aunt is that you get to do all the fun stuff like teach your little nephew how to Vaseline his parents' toilet seat or short-sheet their bed while avoiding all the work like paying for his education or bail money.

The closest I'd come to motherhood was caring for my six-pound Chihuahua. But you can't put your child in a purse and go to a bar. Like Vin Diesel in *The Pacifier*, I was totally unprepared.

For my day of motherhood, Jen invited me to their home, where she promised to remain on hand to coach me and prevent disaster. Although Jen and Hank are relaxed, cool parents, they were smart enough not to leave their infant alone with an inexperienced burnout like myself.

Jen and Hank are both stunning, and as a result, Henry was one of the most adorable babies I had ever seen. Because both parents are tall, Henry was also one of the biggest babies I had ever seen, weighing in at more than twenty pounds. The three-pound barbells I'd been curling did me no good, especially since almost every task of motherhood entails holding your baby in one arm while you do something with the other arm. If you want to get an idea of what caring for an infant is like, try tying an arm behind your back for the entirety of your day. Or better yet, carry an extremely fragile twenty-pound art object in the crook of your arm all day long without dropping it.

"The trick is occupying the child in order to accomplish whatever tasks you have," Jen noted.

Thankfully Henry was easily occupied. After years of performing for disinterested, drunken audiences at open mikes, I found him to be an ideal audience.

"He likes you," Jen said, handing me the behemoth tot and instructing me to place him in the Pack 'n Play. Cribs are totally passé, but the Pack 'n Play is like an infant universe. It is a portable playpen with a canopy, foldout changing table, and diaper bag. An attachment provides ambient bird sounds, water sounds, or music. And the entire Pack 'n Play has a vibrating function! I wondered why any of us still sleep in beds.

In the Pack 'n Play were two little stuffed toys—a bear named "Moosey Bear" and a more abstract smiley-face creature named "Mr. Whosit."

"He loves it when you beat up Mr. Whosit," Jen noted, giving the hapless toy a sound thrashing upon the sides of the Pack 'n Play. Henry smiled beatifically at the mistreatment of Mr. Whosit, as if to say, "This is the best show I've ever seen."

Jen handed me Mr. Whosit, and I took a turn cathartically beating the crap out of him.

I heard Jen fire up a vacuum in the kitchen.

"You shouldn't have to vacuum," I said. "I'm the mom for a day. You go relax."

"I'm not sure I know how to do that," she said.

"Here, let me do it." I took the vacuum from her and quickly realized that vacuums have advanced at the same rate as baby furniture. The last vacuum I used was a leaden Electrolux as old as me, but Jen's vacuum looked like something out of *Starship Troopers*. It was blue and purple and had several baffling attachments and hoses. It could have sucked up a small sofa.

I returned to the Pack 'n Play to fetch Henry for feeding. I hoisted the little dude onto my hip as Jen stood by and explained the complexities of getting Henry into his high-chair. I had to slide the chair's tray out with one hand and with the other place Henry into the chair, keeping a hand on his tummy so he wouldn't fall over while I slid the tray back in.

"It's amazing my mom managed to smoke all those years," I observed. "Where did she get a free hand?"

I secured the infant inside the chair and presented him with the various courses of his meal: a bright pink one that looked like borscht but was actually pears and blueberries, a green one that looked like wheatgrass but was actually blended organic green beans, and a beige organic whole wheat oatmeal course. If adults ate like this, we'd all be much healthier.

"You've got to watch his hands while you're feeding him. He tries to stick his fingers in the food," Jen warned.

"How much should he eat?" I asked.

"All of it."

Apparently the goal of feeding time is to get as much food into the baby's mouth as possible, with no regard for your own dignity. If it takes opening your mouth wide like a jack-ass or pretending the spoon is an aircraft, these are things you must do to ensure your child eats. That is, until the child is old enough for you to induce guilt by referencing "children starving in other countries."

The other goal of feeding is making sure the child's face doesn't become encrusted with food, which will happen if you don't wipe the excess off after each bite. "The wipe is really an art form," Jen told me as I accidentally streaked green bean across Henry's cheek.

Luckily, Henry really likes food, and before long he'd gobbled his meal up like a trucker at a greasy spoon.

"I'm gonna go get the Fun Ultrasaucer," Jen suggested.

She emerged carrying a bright purple contraption.

"I won't be surprised if you build one for yourself," she added.

"It's like a massive trip toy!" I exclaimed, placing Henry's legs through the Saucer's leg holes. The Saucer is designed so that the baby chills like a ringed planet at the Saucer's center. The rings around the baby contain sensory stimuli—sounds, lights, mirrors, rattles, and spinning wheels that make it a "fun ultra" experience.

"I don't know who is designing baby products—" I began.

"But they must be smoking a lot of weed," Jen finished.

"Exactly. Who thought of this? It's genius."

After thoroughly exhausting the Saucer, we headed downstairs for a *Teletubbies* fix, which I looked forward to because watching TV is something I know how to do. Plus I'm a big fan of *Teletubbies*. I was thrilled when Jen told me that Henry also really dug *Teletubbies*. Not surprising, since acid casualties and babies tend to be on the same page aesthetically.

I slid Henry into a Lennon Baby bouncy chair and got ready for quality entertainment.

As Jen scrolled through the channels, I told her about a six-hour *Teletubbies* viewing marathon I'd engaged in with my friend Ennis. At one point, Ennis turned down the sound on the television and turned up Beck's *Odelay*. It looked like the *Teletubbies* were dancing to Beck. It fit more perfectly than *The Wizard of Oz* and *Dark Side of the Moon*. We were amazed by the synchronicity, when suddenly a guitar magically appeared, and Laa-Laa started playing it.

Jen turned on the TV. The episode began and Henry started giggling. It turned out to be the episode I'd just described.

"Look—Tinky Winky hates the music that Laa-Laa is playing, so he puts his hands over his ears and runs away. He probably wants to listen to Cher," I noted.

"He's running away with his purse."

"He's off to Rawhide."

It's sad when you are obviously enjoying an episode of *Teletubbies* more than the infant next to you is enjoying it.

Henry was almost asleep when the episode finished. I carried him upstairs and put him in a swingy chair for a nap. Unlike a bouncy chair, which bounces, a swingy chair rocks gently back and forth, lulling the infant to sleep.

"How can he sleep with all that movement?" I asked.

"It's the movement that helps him sleep."

As Henry snoozed I spoke to Jen about motherhood.

She read to me from a journal she keeps that she'll someday give to Henry when he's old enough to appreciate it. In it, she'd written simple things one might write in a baby book, such as his weight and height. But she also wrote down her fears about current political leaders, war, and the destruction of the environment. It made me realize how terrifying it must be to raise a child in the political shitstorm of the new millennium.

"Do you want to make a bottle?" Jen asked cheerily.

"Sure."

"You use four and a half scoops of this," she said, pointing to formula and a tiny scooper. "Then you add the water and put it in the fridge." I washed my hands and began scooping out the formula, but it only took about five seconds to forget how many scoops I'd poured.

"Wait, was that three or four? I can't remember."

"Just pour it out and start over."

Little noises emanated from the swingy chair. Henry had woken and he was crying. I picked him up and held him.

"Shhhh, it's okay," I cooed softly. I tried to convince him

that it really was okay, but he was eyeing his actual mother. I felt like I was exploiting him for the sake of science. Although I've felt this way many times, I always continued because those I exploited were usually embittered adults like me. But when a perfect five-month-old wants his mama, you've got to give him that.

I handed him to Jen and the crying ceased immediately.

After a spell, she passed him back to me, and we ventured into the kitchen to make a bottle of apple juice, which luckily involved no mixing, measuring, or short-term memory. Resting Henry on my hip, I twisted open the bottle and poured the juice inside.

"You're a natural," Jen observed.

"Yeah, but I'm uncoordinated," I said, struggling to twist the bottle closed.

I sat down on the couch with Henry on my lap.

"Ooh, I think somebody did a stinky," Jen suddenly remarked.

She must have a nose like a bloodhound, because I could smell nothing.

I'd been hoping I'd get through the day without a diaper ordeal, but it was bound to happen. I flipped open the Pack 'n Play's changing table and held my breath. Luckily, the many years I spent as a swimmer have enabled me to go for long periods of time without breathing through my nose.

That said, no matter how many Baby Alive dolls you played with as a child, little can prepare you for real diaper changing, wherein you are forced to actually wipe shit off another human's ass. And regardless of how cute and little the human whose ass you're wiping is, it's still pretty damn gross.

Jen instructed me to take Henry's feet with one hand and lift his butt up, whereupon I was to remove the diaper and baby-wipe the ass clean with the other hand. I held his feet and lifted gently.

"You're not gonna break him," she said.

I put a little muscle into it, hoisted him up, and slid off the diaper.

"Oh, that's not a bad one," Jen said, pooh-poohing my horror.

"If that's not a bad one, I don't want to see a bad one."

Several baby wipes later, he was fresh and clean as an Irish spring, and I was humbled by the thought that long ago my mother had been just as grossed out by my diapers as I had been by Henry's.

17 REAR WINDOW

FACEBOY AND I smoked opium for the first time, and all I could say was, "This is the best thing in the world. We need to get more of this."

"Rev., that's how entire civilizations have been destroyed."

"Oh yeah, we can never do this again."

The opium was the only thing that cheered me up that November.

My memoir was complete. I'd gotten an agent who took it around and sent it to the publishers in London, but no one wanted it. My heart sank. If I could have climbed inside that opium pipe and stayed there for the rest of the winter, I would have.

My skin was broken out, my belly distended. Gray hairs popped up everywhere. If I hadn't still been shaving my vagina they probably would've popped up there too.

Anthony had sent me exactly one letter, which I couldn't read because his handwriting was so bad. Friends tried to interpret it, but all anyone could make out were a few lines about drinking tea and morning erections.

And it was getting cold. There was no heat in my apartment, so I bought a space heater, which JJ and I huddled around. After one hour, it blew every fuse in the building. My slumlords were gutting the apartment next to mine and a family of mice had decided to move into my apartment and not pay rent. They were adorable, but JJ cried when they stole food from her dish right in front of her.

I felt like a total failure, living hand-to-mouth with no money, no health insurance, no savings, and no plan. The city marshals called and threatened to take away my property because of my outstanding debt to the hospital from when my appendix ruptured. I told them I had no property. I wanted to declare bankruptcy but couldn't afford it. About the only thing I could afford was one twelve-ounce can of Budweiser, and another, and another . . .

So it seemed appropriate for my next column to be about getting fucked in the ass.

The few times I'd tried anal intercourse lasted less than five minutes and ended with me leaping off the bed in pain. But I was sure that with a little effort it might be something I could enjoy. I'd been a doubter going into the squirting column, and now I couldn't keep my fingers off my G-spot.

Plus my asshole would be tagging along throughout my entire life, so I figured it should be in on the fun. My vagina and clit received an inordinate amount of attention, but my anus was like an awkward middle child who only got noticed when acting up.

Like Lewis and Clark's survey of uncharted territory, my rectal exploration required supplies, equipment, and manpower. I began with a copy of *Anal Pleasure and Health*. Published in 1981, it was the first comprehensive source of information on the subject. The first chapter, "Anal Pleasure and the Anal Taboo," deals with existing attitudes toward the anus. Author Jack Morin explains that many people are alienated from their assholes or think of them as dirty and disgusting.

But I belong to a community of free spirits! I thought. I witness performance artists pulling produce out of their orifices on a regular basis. Surely there is no anal taboo among us. And yet, when I revealed my plans for anal action, many behaved as though I'd just declared an interest in scat. One friend called such an undertaking "gross." I realized that even amongst the liberated, there is shame about the asshole.

Luckily, some friends were supportive.

"I'm for anal the way I'm for the underdog," my friend, Margaret said. "I don't like to see anything dismissed or maligned just out of ignorance or fear."

I was more determined than ever to enjoy my asshole, if only to uphold its glory in the face of those who maligned it. Natalie lent me her autographed copy of *The Ultimate Guide to Anal Sex for Women.*

My own exploration began with the fourth chapter of *Anal Pleasure and Health*, "Looking and Touching." Using a hand mirror and plenty of light, I bent over and examined my anus. It looked like a set of pursed lips that never smiled. I felt sorry for it.

"Also in your journal, consider using a pencil, crayons, or colored pencils to draw a picture of your anus," Jack Morin suggests. Because I'm used to drawing from life, I tried bending over and sketching my anus at the same time, but found it too difficult. Putting the mirror down, I rendered my anus from memory and proudly hung the drawing on my wall.

I returned to the mirror, took another look, and slowly

touched my anus. "Imagine how mom and dad might feel if they knew what you were doing," the book proposed.

An image of my mother crying popped into my head. My father tried to comfort her, saying, "At least she has a job." The book encourages anal explorers to write an imaginary letter to their parents explaining what they are doing and why. I skipped the letter. If I had to write an imaginary letter for every action I performed that my parents would deem disturbing, I'd never get anything done.

For a few days I followed Jack Morin's instructions for getting to know my ass. I became more aware of my anal muscles and was able to contract and relax them voluntarily during moments of boredom.

Anal Pleasure and Health covers an immense amount of ground: anal tension, anal hygiene, analingus, homophobia, STDs, even the effects of Quaaludes and the two main rules of anal sex: never put anything in your pussy that's just been in your ass; and never have unprotected sex with anyone unless you're in a monogamous relationship.

After all that, it was time to actually stick something up my ass. I headed over to Babeland in search of a butt toy. There I found the Stealth plug, a vibrating instrument the size of a large man's finger. Its military-inspired packaging featured an image of a jet fighter.

At the checkout, a man was buying a harness, a dildo, and lube. Next to his large dildo, my commando butt plug didn't seem so impressive. I smiled at him. We were the only two customers in the store and we were both looking to pleasure our asses.

I rushed home and examined the plug. Considering it has a white cord (making it look a little like an iPod) and attached battery pack, it really isn't so stealthy. But it does vibrate silently.

Because the Stealth is made of jelly rubber, I draped a condom over it and slicked it up with lube. Breathing deeply, I relaxed my ass and slowly inserted the plug. I lay back on my bed and closed my eyes, conjuring an image of Robert Plant circa 1970. When my kitty grew moist, I flipped the switch to vibrate. Nothing happened.

Of course—toys never include batteries. It's one of the only certainties in life, right after death and taxes. Because my hands were covered in lube, I wondered how I was ever going to slide open the battery hatch. The Stealth certainly felt good and I was in no mood to remove it, but I wondered how I was going to make it to the kitchen for batteries with a butt plug cord dangling from my anus without my roommate seeing me. *I could just masturbate,* I thought. But no, I had a vibrating butt plug; I wanted it to vibrate. Hastily, I grabbed my television's remote control and transferred its batteries to the Stealth—not realizing the Stealth was turned to the highest setting. I got quite a surprise when it began vibrating at full throttle.

Once my shock subsided, I enjoyed the sensation of anal vibration. It was like having a rectal massage. I'm guessing the difference between a normal butt plug and a vibrating butt plug is like the difference between Stove Top and homemade stuffing.

I massaged my clit and came quickly, then lay on my bed immobilized, staring at the drawing of my anus on the wall.

If anal sex—the accurate term for all forms of anal pleasure—is college, then anal intercourse (butt-fucking) is graduation. (Fisting is like grad school.) Now that I'd learned to take pleasure in the Stealth plug, it was time to give a penis a whirl. For this step, I needed a partner. I hadn't had sex—vaginal, anal, or otherwise—in a while, but I knew that when in need, I could call Orion.

The great thing about Erin and Orion, other than their absolute willingness to take part in my experiments, was the lack of drama involved. I knew Orion would fuck me in the ass and leave if I asked him to.

Only problem was that Orion was well-hung. I could have chosen a man with a tiny penis, but I wasn't about to cheat just to make my lab easier. I had to want my lab partner. Desire is the single most important element in anal sex. If you don't want it, it'll never work. While the vagina is elastic enough to take a penis even if the woman is making a mental grocery list, it's much harder for an asshole to lie. It will close up like a frightened clam at any hint of unwanted intrusion.

And I knew that if I told Orion to stop, he wouldn't try to ram it in like a porn star.

He arrived at midnight after a daylong drinking bender. I was also mildly inebriated and exhausted. Both books advocate sobriety when engaging in anal intercourse, presumably so the recipient doesn't awaken with a torn-up asshole, confused.

We started off with a bit of harmless looking and touching, but when it came time for finger insertion I realized I'd misplaced my bottle of lube.

"I swear it was right next to my bed," I said, turning over furniture and rifling through my underwear drawer.

We sat on the edge of my bed while Orion marveled at the colorful panties I'd flung around him.

"How does one lose an entire bottle of lube?" I said. "I really need to clean my room."

We opted to experiment with analingus instead.

I felt a little self-conscious about having another human's face buried in my ass. *Do I smell fresh?* I wondered, but heard no complaints from Orion, who later admitted to enjoying it more than he'd anticipated.

We switched places and I got to work rimming Orion. It was difficult to tell whether I was getting him off, because all I could see was his asshole. I suppose I could have lifted my head up to see if he looked bored or excited, but I was too focused. There was certainly nothing gross about licking Orion's ass. He tasted clean and a little salty.

But I will say that analingus is completely unromantic—long walks on the beach, candlelit dinners, and ass-licking just don't go together.

After we grew tired of analingus, we made a date for the following Friday. Orion suggested we strap the lube to my forearm.

When Friday rolled around, I went back to Babeland and acquired the video companion to *The Ultimate Guide to Anal Sex for Women*, thinking it might inspire us. Later that day, Orion arrived at my door, carrying a bottle of lube and a copy of Toni Bentley's *The Surrender: an Erotic Memoir*, stolen by Erin. *The Surrender* is the memoir of a former ballerina who discovers her love of anal sex. Erin earmarked her favorite sections, which Orion and I read aloud. In a section entitled "The Box," the author describes a lacquered box where she keeps her collection of used condoms. In another section, we discovered she'd been boned in the ass 298 times by her lover. In "Profile of an Ass Fucker," she describes her lover as being "the least annoying" man she's ever known.

"Wow, she sums it up there," I noted. "If you want to fuck someone in the ass, it's really important not to annoy them."

I put the book down and started the video. It begins with John "Buttman" Stagliano challenging Tristan Taormino to pop a porn star's anal cherry. With the help of a magic wand and a twirling vibrator, she rises to the challenge.

"I've never seen a vibrator twirl like that!" Orion exclaimed.

"I used to have a vibrator like that, but I had to throw it out," I said, sighing.

"Why?"

"I wasn't getting any work done."

"This is actually sort of hot," Orion said.

"I know," I said. "I'm kind of ready to get started."

We managed to watch a few more scenes, including one in which a lovely lady named Jazmine takes her porn star boyfriend Nacho's penis inside her ass for the first time.

"Wow, he knew what he was going to do with the rest of his life when he hit puberty," Orion noted as Nacho dropped his pants, revealing an enormous penis.

Nacho warmed Jazmine's ass up with his fingers, anal beads, a dildo, clitoral stimulation, and vaginal intercourse before finally taking her in the ass.

Orion and I turned our attention away from the TV.

"Let's do it," I said.

"Yeah, why watch it when you can live it?"

I lubed up the Stealth and inserted it while Orion kissed and caressed me. Any physical exertion should always involve a warm-up, and anal intercourse is no different. We started with a little old-fashioned vaginal intercourse. Orion slipped on a condom and entered me while I still bore the Stealth plug. The feeling of fullness was incredible. Orion held the Stealth's switch in his hand and played with the various levels of vibration while he moved in and out of me, slow and low.

I was getting too excited.

Orion pulled out and removed his condom. I gave him a little oral while manually keeping up my own level of arousal.

I lifted my head from his loins and bit my lip. "Go slow," I said. He already knew this, but I felt a last-minute need to reiterate. I removed the Stealth and applied half a bottle of lube to my asshole while Orion donned another condom. I got on all fours, and Orion entered me slower than a three-toed sloth with a bad leg. As Jack Morin pointed out, often partners must try several positions before they find one that's compatible with the shape of their rectum. For some reason, doggie-style just wasn't working.

I turned over and lay on my back, lifting up my legs. Orion got on top and slowly entered me. This time it as was smooth as butter. He was all the way in, and it didn't hurt. I couldn't believe it.

"Are you actually inside my ass?" I asked. "I'm not implying that you have a small penis or anything; it's just that it doesn't hurt. It feels great. I never expected missionary position and anal sex to go together."

I thrust toward him and he moaned.

"How do you like being inside my ass?" I asked.

"It's incredible," he said.

"Is it tight?"

"Yes."

We moved together like this for several minutes until I spied my Nubby G vibrator next to the bed. I placed it against my clit and turned it on, then slid the tip inside my vagina.

"I can feel it vibrate on my cock," Orion said.

We continued like this for a while. It felt amazing, but for some reason neither of us came. Maybe we were too nervous.

Eventually, I had to take a break, not because my ass hurt, but because my legs had been over my earlobes for a good twenty minutes and I had to pee. Orion pulled out and we lay on the bed, ecstatic that we hadn't injured or disappointed each other. I caressed my asshole with my fingertips. It was open and relaxed.

"Look at my asshole," I said, showing off. "It's not like pursed lips anymore. It's smiling."

18

SEX AND THE CITY ENDURANCE TEST

I'D BEEN WRITING the column for a year and had grown a little tired of having sex.

The same thing happened when I worked at a pizza place and got tired of eating pizza. (It only took a few weeks of not working at the pizza place for me to enjoy pizza again, and I hoped the same thing would happen with sex.)

Perhaps Michael Martin sensed I needed a break from boning when he assigned my next column. A new DVD set of the complete *Sex and the City* episodes had just been released. Michael suggested I watch every episode in a row.

"Like a *Sex and the City* endurance test," he said.

I love TV, maybe even more than pizza or sex. And I had been deprived of cable television for most of my adult life, so I was never exposed to *Sex and the City* fever. For the most part, I was busy watching Charlie Rose explore the human genome project while Midwestern soccer moms watched Carrie Bradshaw weigh the pros and cons of golden showers. Now I could finally catch up.

The *Sex and the City* endurance test was almost canceled when my clout as a Nerve columnist proved insufficient to procure the $299.95 DVD set for free. Luckily, Nerve's Date DVD columnist, Logan Hill, agreed to lend me his copy.

When Logan handed me the weighty set, I marveled at its fancy packaging. The nineteen discs come in a pink velvet book encased in its own lucite box. Within the book are synopses of each episode, like CliffsNotes for TV.

Because of my part-time job at the bookstore, holiday plans, and travel, the only realistic time to begin my experiment was at dawn on a Thursday morning. If I started at night, the risk of falling asleep would be too great. When I awoke at 5:30 AM and informed the dude next to me in bed that I was about to watch ninety-six episodes of *Sex and the City*, he put on his pants and fled from my boudoir faster than Wally West. Apparently *Sex and the City* is about as popular among straight men as the *American Outdoorsman* is among women.

Earlier, friends had shared input regarding the experiment. Faceboy offered tips used by amateur radio broadcasters for staying awake during emergency operations. These included eating only high-carb, low-fat, and high-protein snacks, avoiding large, heavy meals, and drinking lots of water. He added that sleep is induced by a low body temperature. If you need to stay awake, it's best to keep the environment warm, between seventy-two and seventy-four degrees—though he conceded that the last point is kind of irrelevant in ghetto apartments like mine, where there is never sufficient heat.

His advice was sound, but I opted for other methods, tested during a little sleep-deprivation exercise I call "my twenties." These methods include the use of caffeine, sugar, and just the right mix of cold medicine and pot. I walked JJ to Dunkin' Donuts, where I grabbed a large "turbo" coffee. This, coupled with eyedrops and Advil Cold & Sinus, unpeeled my eyelids from my cheekbones. The sun wasn't up yet and the hipsters were just beginning their arduous walks-of-shame home. Waking up early just to watch TV made me feel like a child waking up early for Saturday-morning cartoons. If, when I was six, someone told me that in twenty-seven years I'd get to watch TV for fifty hours, I would have been psyched.

At home, I placed my laptop beside me on the bed along with two remote controls—one for my pink "Princess TV" and one for my DVD player. Throwing on a pair of oversized pajamas, I climbed under the covers and began with disc one, season one.

The following is a record of what happened:

THURSDAY, 7 AM

Season one introduces the show's protagonist, Carrie, played by Sarah Jessica Parker. Carrie is a thirty-something, boy-crazy, sexual anthropologist *just like me!* But the similarities seem to end there. She lives on the Upper East Side. I live on the Lower East Side. She buys $400 shoes. I buy socks at the ninety-nine-cent store. Yet I'm already daydreaming about my TV show. Who would play me? One of the Olsen twins? That would fit nicely with the child-star-turned-cable-TV-star trend. Speaking of which, it's 1998 in season one and Carrie's style is still a little *Square Pegs*. I'm growing nostalgic for the last millennium. Little backpacks and giant cell phones don't seem so bad when compared to monthly natural disasters and a lunatic president. Carrie not only smokes onscreen, you could still smoke in New York City bars back then.

7:30 AM

Only ninety-four episodes to go! Carrie is stuck on an a-hole named Mr. Big. He blows smoke up her ass when he tells her, "There are so many goddamned gorgeous women in this city, but after a while you just wanna be with one that makes you laugh." I've heard that line. Maybe straight men hate this show because it portrays them as the evil svengalis they often are. Either that, or they're depicted as needy and weak like Carrie's friend, Skipper.

8:30 AM

Samantha, Carrie's "loose" friend, bones a hot Irish doorman. The sight of his nubile, pasty chest is arousing. This show is actually jack-off material for straight women.

9 AM

Do people in Nebraska think this is how New Yorkers live? The women on this show work about as much as Mr. Rogers. Miranda, Carrie's nerdy friend, is supposedly a high-powered attorney, but I've yet to see her do a stitch of work. They all have jobs, but they spend most of their time just hangin' out and shootin' the shit. No one in New York has this much time on their hands except for socialites. Even so, I like the show.

Carrie and Samantha are boning twenty-something men. This is a phenomenon that's taken hold of my thirty-something friends lately, so I can relate. The club Torch is featured in this episode. Torch was once a happening club in my neighborhood until, fittingly, it burned down. Once I tried to gain entry there while wearing a Teletubby costume and was refused on the grounds that I had no I.D.

11 AM

I'm still *really* enjoying the show, though it unrealistically depicts Carrie typing her column in a tube top and full makeup. If readers saw what I look like when I'm typing, I'd never get laid again. Episode eight asks the question, "Are three-ways the blowjobs of the '90s?" Now that it's 2006, I'll have to say they were. I had two three-ways in the '90s, though I was drinking a lot more back then.

Carrie sleeps with Mr. Big on the first date. Now he's withholding and cold. It's like watching a mirror image of myself. I don't learn from my mistakes. Maybe I'll learn from Carrie's.

NOON

I start sobbing because Carrie is unable to date "the new Yankee" because of her misguided love for Big.

My friend Tanya, a fellow art star, calls. I say, "Please come over. I'm lonely."

"Is it okay if we take a *Passions* break at two?" she asks.

"I can't take a break," I say. "Come after *Passions* ."

2 PM

I eat a pot cookie. I was only going to eat half, but then I thought, *mmm, a cookie.* Boy, am I stoned. Perfect timing. Carrie is wearing a holographic tube top and it's more psychedelic than *Laser Floyd: Dark Side of the Moon.* At first I think maybe she's topless and they're blurring out her boobs. I wonder why she's topless in a restaurant. Then I realize it's a tube top.

2:30 PM

Miranda and her boyfriend, Steve, are eating pizza. I would kill for a slice. I cry a second time when Big takes a cell phone call while Carrie is reading a poem at a friend's wedding.

4 PM

Tanya called and asked if I needed anything. "Pizza . . . and hurry!" I begged. Now she is here. I am happy to have human contact and food. Tanya is a well-informed fan of the show.

"How can she afford an Upper East Side apartment on a writer's salary?" I ask.

"It's rent-controlled and costs only $750 a month," Tanya says.

"My apartment is cheaper than that."

"See, you could be living a life of Manolo Blahniks and you didn't even know it."

"You know what's weird? This all happened before internet dating. People still met in bars."

"And yet they manage to be so slutty without the help of internet dating."

"True. It was tough back then."

5:30 PM

Tom arrives with a twenty-four-ounce Budweiser. I know I should stay away from downers, but I've been on an emotional roller-coaster with this Carrie-and-Big nonsense. Big makes Carrie cry again. I say, "She's a really good actress. Look at her, she's really crying."

Tanya asks, "How long have you been watching this?"

"Since 6 AM."

"I think you need to see *Somewhere Tomorrow*."

"God, I have to pee again. I should be wearing diapers," I moaned. Though I've been fast-forwarding through the theme song, my constant need to pee is slowing down the marathon.

"Episode twenty-three!" I triumphantly announce.

Tom trumps my boast by telling me he's on episode eighty of *Buffy the Vampire Slayer*. "And that's voluntary," he adds.

6 PM

Now that people are getting off work, they're all stopping by to see me. It's a lot like being a patient in the hospital during visiting hours.

Is this prep work for when the experiment lands me in a mental institution? They come bearing candy, beer, and chips. Monica, Brer Brian, Jim, Tanya, Michelle, Jennifer, Bruce, and Lopi are all here. Tom has to leave.

7:30 PM

Poor Miranda. The stylists really made her look like a dowdy member of the royal family.

"What are you doing with your hair, Miranda?" Tanya taunts the screen. "It looks like a boy's regular."

8:30 PM

Am I going to get bedsores from this? Maybe someone should roll me over. I might as well be watching *Satyricon*. The episodes stopped making sense long ago. The big flower-pin trend is in full swing and it's making me angry. Were the stylists playing a trick on viewers? Jennifer fashions a giant flower out of Budweiser rings.

Next to my bed there's a nail file, Chloraseptic, two phones, a humidifier, and stationery . . . why do I need stationery? Am I planning on staying here for months?

Bruce sits on the remote, momentarily turning the TV off, and everyone starts screaming. We recovered the remote from under his ass and things are back on track.

Aidan, Carrie's new "good" boyfriend, runs a bath for her, and everyone coos.

9:30 PM

Everyone agrees that Aidan is good. He's a carpenter (like Jesus), and when he says to Carrie, "You make me happy," I get a total clit boner.

There are eight people in my bedroom right now. Four of them are on my bed, and we're all watching TV. This seems wrong. "Are you okay?" I ask my friend Brian, who's been totally silent.

"Yeah. I'm just enjoying the show," he says, staring ahead with glazed eyes.

Aha! Straight men pretend to dislike the show, but in reality they probably get more out of it than women. It's research for them.

As Monica points out, "They say they hate it, but if you put it on, they don't move from the couch."

10 PM

I've developed a bump on my finger from the remote control. This is the first sign of physical deterioration I've come across. I don't want any more beer. Has *Sex and the City* cured my problem drinking?

11 PM

I feel like a combination of Howard Hughes, Gertrude Stein, and Brian Wilson: Howard Hughes because I haven't left my apartment, Gertrude Stein because I'm hosting a salon, and Brian Wilson because I'm still wearing my pajamas. At what point do I start actually thinking I *am* Gertrude Stein? Is this the onset of schizophrenia?

MIDNIGHT

Jen, Monica, and Michelle leave. I ask Bruce, "Who would you most like to do?"

"Well, Samantha circa *Mannequin*, and if that's not an option, Miranda."

Despite the fact that the stylists have done their best to make her heinous, Miranda's got the geeky girl thing going. She's also the most bitter of the bunch, which endears her to artists.

1 AM

It's just Lopi, Bruce, and me. It's official: Bruce is the only living person who loves TV as much as I do. Lopi grew up on a hippie commune so TV is still something new to her. I've started to lose my voice.

"How does a person lose their voice just from watching TV?" Lopi asks.

Carrie is dating a comic-book-store guy, but it's the most ridiculous casting ever because he looks like a male model.

Lopi keeps threatening to leave, but because I fast-forward through the theme song, she stays. It gives her no time in between episodes to make a run for it before the next one sucks her in. She says that it's like crack, never having done crack.

Bruce agrees, having done crack.

1:30 AM

Lopi has a freakout. It happens during a scene in which Samantha's doing PR for a thirteen-year-old girl's bat mitzvah. "I can't handle this!" Lopi screams. "These people are not real . . . they can't be!" She throws on her coat and runs out the door screaming.

2 AM

I can barely comment on the horrible outfits anymore, my voice is so gone. Bruce and I almost fade, but then Carrie wears an outfit so bad, it reignites our fascination. It's a neon, patterned leggings-and-oversized-shirt ensemble. Bruce starts shrieking when it comes on the screen, reducing us to fits of hysterical laughter. My stomach hurts from laughing. Then Bruce points out that the outfit is Chanel! I don't believe him until he goes up to the TV and points to the tiny Chanel logo on her chest. Coco must be rolling in her grave.

3 AM

Bruce leaves. His equilibrium is destroyed. He falls over trying to walk through the kitchen. My roommate snaps some photos of me on his digital camera. When we look at them, we laugh uncontrollably. I look horrible, like I've just been on a meth bender. There are crumbs in my tangled hair, and the bags under my eyes are enormous.

3:30 AM

My roommate goes out wearing red eyelashes and glitter. Now I know why the surrealists experimented with sleep deprivation.

4 AM

The fabric of reality has crumbled. I have thoughts, only they're narrated by Sarah Jessica Parker. She's in my head. Charlotte's husband can't get it up.

4:15 AM

I'm getting back under the covers.

FRIDAY, 6 PM

Getting under the covers was a big mistake. I just now woke up to the sound of the show's theme song booming out of my TV. Still, I need closure. Either that, or *Sex and the City* really is like crack. Though I've watched for twenty-two hours, two seasons remain. I need to know what happens to my TV friends. I skip to the last two episodes, hoping things will still make sense.

Carrie is about to move to Paris with her artist boy-friend, played by Mikhail Baryshnikov (who's lookin' good). But the night before her plane leaves, Big shows up. Predictable, yes, but it hit a note. She tells him, "Too little, too late." How many times have I uttered those exact words to the Mr. Bigs of my life? Soon I was crying harder than when Fonzie visited Pinky Tuscadero in the hospital. The sobbing only got worse when I discovered Samantha was going through chemo for breast cancer.

Carrie goes to Paris, and Mikhail turns out to be a total dickhead. She is lonely and misses the people and city she loves.

Meanwhile, Big has resolved to get Carrie back. Scrambling for just how to go about doing it, he faces the tribunal of her friends. "You guys are the loves of her life and a guy is just happy to come in fourth," he tells them. I think about how much I love my friends and how much I love New York and I cry harder. In fact, I sob for the entire last two episodes.

Big goes to Paris, where he declares his love for Carrie, and the two live happily ever after.

It's now been a full twenty-four hours since I stopped watching the show, but Sarah Jessica Parker's voice hasn't left my head. I continually eye the pink velvet book containing the remaining unseen episodes. My desire to watch even more is either a testament to the greatness of *Sex and the City* or evidence of my unwavering love of television. Could this be the start of a terrible TV marathon addiction? Will the Gilmore Girls be next?

19   FIRST BASE

LIKE MOST ADULTS, my New Year's Eves began to suck around the time I started expecting anything from them but watching the ball drop with Dick Clark.

But as 2005 came to an end, Kat announced she was throwing an "Old Hollywood" themed New Year's Eve party. And if there's one thing I can't resist, it's putting on a crazy costume.

"You have to dress as Grusinskaya," Kat commanded. She and her BF, Jesse, had recently seen *Grand Hotel* and were struck by my likeness to the aging, suicidal, ballerina character played by Greta Garbo. In the film, Garbo makes her famous pronouncement, "I want to be alone," before falling madly in love with a gentleman jewel thief named Baron Felix von Geigern, played by John Barrymore. Shortly thereafter, the Baron is murdered, leaving Garbo's character exactly where she started: alone.

My life was about to play out in a similar fashion.

Daniel was twenty-six, six and a half feet tall, with light

green eyes, full lips, golden ringlets, and a body like Wolverine. When he walked into a room, vaginas immediately moistened. He was an actor and a singer in a rockin' band that hung out at the Anti-Slam. I refused to have a crush on him, precisely because he was so beautiful. It disgusted me the way women fawned over him. After all, he was just a dude.

Despite my unwillingness to consciously incorporate him into my repertoire of jack-off material, one night I dreamt that we made love. I woke up on the brink of orgasm.

The night before I left for London, he walked me home from a show and gave me a long kiss goodbye on my doorstep. I didn't invite him up because I thought he was only being polite. When he showed up at the New Year's party, I expected him to kiss someone much hotter and younger than me at midnight. Especially since I looked like a freak in my clownish Garbo makeup.

Little did I know he would approach me, stealthy as a gentleman jewel thief.

"How 'bout a New Year's kiss, Rev. Jen?" he asked.

I kissed him.

His lips were like two giant pillows that my lips wanted to sleep on forever.

We spent the night kissing, never reaching second base. It had been so long since anyone had just wanted to kiss me, I kept waiting for him to ask me to give him analingus or to pee on him. In fact, on my way to the party, I'd run into a fellow who suggested I fuck him in the ass with a dildo "for science." Being a sex columnist meant romance was hard to come by.

For the next couple of weeks, I made out with Daniel

every time I saw him—at parties, at open mikes, and in the backseat of his drummer's car. I wondered if he'd ever try to touch my boobs.

Then one day he told me he'd been cast in a TV pilot and had to leave for Los Angeles right away. The night before he left, he came over and made love to me. It was better than it had been in my dream.

The next day, I figured I would never see him again. I'd learned from previous lovers: *Los Angeles is the Bermuda Triangle of men.* They go, and they never return.

20 LUBE GIRL

I AM NOT a huge fan of porn. Given the choice between porn and reruns of *Charles in Charge*, I'd probably opt for the latter. Most adult films appear to rely on a predictable L.A. formula: Barbie gets banged by Ken while both recite trite banter referencing either the size of Ken's manhood or the tightness of Barbie's holes. All of that happens on a shoddily art-directed set with no plot and bad makeup. Either that, or it's too softcore, like watching a *Lifetime* original movie with exposed nipples.

But while porn bores me, porn *stars* fascinate me. Most people spend their whole lives trying to please their parents, whereas porn stars are people who've openly given up. They're kind of like people with facial tattoos.

I figured if I worked on the set of a porno for a day, I would get to meet porn stars. Plus I would gain experience for future filmmaking endeavors.

The only problem was that I was stuck in New York. And trying to find a porn director in New York is like looking for a scuba instructor in Kansas. Most porn comes out of L.A., a city that attracts actors who *want* to fuck on film. New York attracts performers who want to sing Billy Joel songs on Broadway or star in off-off Broadway productions about their vaginas. Hence the pickings are slim.

Velocity had just returned from the AVN Awards in Vegas (the "Oscars of Adult") where she met Joe Gallant, who runs Black Mirror Productions, a New York–based porn production company. She suggested I contact him.

I sent Joe an email requesting clothed work on one of his films.

"No problem, Jen, baby. Call my cell," he responded.

I called Joe and we chatted. Given my TV production experience and my writing credit on *Lord of the Cockrings*, I was hired.

The shoot for Black Mirror's latest production, *Anal NYC*, was to begin the following day at LIT, an East Village dive bar. Joe invited me to a party at LIT that evening for the cast and crew.

If you recall the pool party in *Boogie Nights*, then try to imagine its *opposite*, you'll have some idea of what this party was like. LIT was dark. Everyone was clothed, and the hardest drug anyone was doing was Budweiser.

"You're adorable, Rev. Why don't you do porn?" Joe asked.

"Because I still believe I'm going to be America's sweetheart and that someday I'll win an Emmy."

"Well, you could always fluff," he suggested.

"I've been warned not to fluff."

"Honestly, since Viagra came along, fluffers aren't really used so much."

Apparently, Viagra is to porn what the cotton gin was to the textile industry.

"Well, we should collaborate on something," he added. "Maybe you can help think of the plot setup for tomorrow's shoot."

I looked around LIT. Short of a million-dollar budget, a team of art directors, or Thom Filicia from *Queer Eye for the Straight Guy*, there was no way to disguise the fact that LIT was a grungy bar. One of the challenges of filming any movie in New York City is finding decent places to shoot. Real estate is so hard to come by here that residents have taken to living in storage units.

"Well, there's no way we can make this place look like anything but a bar, so all of the action will have to take place in a bar," I noted.

Having spent half of my adult life in East Village bars, I knew I would be the perfect script supervisor.

"Who are the stars?" I asked.

"Tyla Wynn, who just won an AVN award for best performance in a three-way—she's flying in from L.A. tonight."

"How hardcore is this movie?" I asked.

"Well, Tyla's prepared to take a good, hard pounding, but it's pretty mainstream compared to a lot of my stuff."

Maybe the *real* reason I've never done porn is that I'm not prepared to take a "good, hard pounding."

Joe explained that *Anal NYC* is a series of vignettes, which only required a simple setup.

"Maybe she could be auditioning him for a band. He could be a drummer," I suggested.

Joe liked that.

I blurted out a list of scenarios. One involved a slumming socialite who loses a contact lens on the street.

"How does she lose a contact?" Joe asked.

"Maybe a tumbleweed hits her in the face. We could show footage of a tumbleweed blowing across the desert. Then we could cut to her saying, 'A tumbleweed just hit me in my face!' We could jump on the *Brokeback Mountain* craze by showing two cowboys blowing each other on the prairie. That's what sets the tumbleweed in motion. The socialite then wanders into the bar with blurred vision, where the bar-back seduces her."

This idea was scrapped. In porn, directors like to keep it simple. I'd developed ten minutes of exposition before the main characters started fucking.

"Maybe I can just be the official *lube girl*?" I offered. "I'll make sure everyone's got enough lube."

"Perfect."

As we discussed further plot ideas, a blond porn star named Heather Pink arrived, escorted by her boyfriend. Heather wore heels and a fur-trimmed coat. Her boyfriend wore a turtleneck and jaunty scarf, like Alexander Cabot III from *Josie and the Pussycats*. They looked like real porn people. Shortly thereafter I left, satisfied that I'd met at least one porn star.

The next day I arrived on set wearing a purple, dragon-emblazoned mini-dress, just in case a cameo was called for. Joe stood outside with Tyla, a bubbly blonde with an ass you could play Jenga on. Her hip-hugger jeans revealed a sliver of crack. It was hard for me, and the rest of Second Avenue, not to stare.

"We need to get enemas," Joe pronounced. "Wanna come?"

Already I was faced with a gritty reality of porn.

"I'm taking no chances. I'm getting a six-pack," Joe declared in the drug store, holding up the economy pack of enemas. From there he hit the lube aisle. "Astroglide—second only to nature," he stated, procuring a bottle.

I'm sure that in L.A., directors have production assistants who buy lube and enemas for them, but New York isn't quite so highbrow. Also in L.A. you'd have to drive three miles to find a pharmacy. I was reminded of why I love New York: you can get a bottle of lube, a slice of pizza, and a psychic reading all on one block.

On the way back, Joe explained the scene's setup. Tyla would play a DJ and Johnny Castle a prospective employee arriving for a DJ audition. When Johnny finds the position has been filled, he must prove he's talented in other fields, like "putting it in."

Back at LIT, Tyla was trying to decide what to wear.

"You could wear one of my T-shirts," Joe said, handing her a shirt promoting his movie "Potty Mouth." Tyla suggested it be cut in a more risqué manner.

"Can you run to the store and get some scissors?" Joe asked me. "You'll get wardrobe credit."

"Really?" I was excited, though it wasn't like I'd be getting a wardrobe credit in a Merchant Ivory period piece. I'd be getting a credit in a movie where the actors are naked ninety-eight percent of the time.

At the deli next door, all I could find was an "emergency sewing kit" that contained the tiniest pair of scissors ever produced. I doubted they could even cut through paper, but it *was* an emergency, and at ninety-nine cents it wouldn't break the production's bank. Back on set, everyone got a kick out of watching Joe try to saw through fabric with the ridiculous scissors before giving up. I was sent back outside, where I finally found a decent pair of scissors.

Once Tyla was in her now-teensy shirt and jeans, Johnny Castle arrived. He looked like a jock. Together he and Tyla looked like the type of people who called me an art fag in high school. Actually, Tyla looked like she was *still* in high school.

The stars asked for beer. Joe handed me some money and instructed me to get water and beer and to make copies of release forms. I couldn't believe I was being entrusted with another task after the scissors fiasco. This time I didn't fail.

Joe filmed the opening sequence in three takes, and the crew moved into the bar's greenroom to shoot the sex scenes. Suddenly a dozen people materialized. There were two photographers, a couple of random dudes, a woman named Simone, a Canadian TV crew, and Keith, who was videotaping Joe.

"Should I get the lube?" I asked Joe.

"The lube's already in her butt."

The camera rolled and Tyla sauntered in, leading Johnny to a ripped pleather couch. Spoiler alert: *she gave him a blow-job*. He then performed cunnilingus. Here, she ad-libbed some dialogue. Grabbing his hand, she licked his fingers. "Let me taste that fucking pussy. Let me taste it right off your fucking hand."

Joe held a light in one hand and the camera in the other, zooming in close for the beaver shot.

Johnny and Tyla then wasted no time putting the anal in *Anal NYC*. I felt a little uncomfortable watching two strangers have anal sex only a few feet away. I thought if they looked over I should give them the thumbs-up or show some sign of encouragement. But they never looked at me. In fact, they didn't really look at each other. I wondered if the dudes in the room were sporting wood. I tried to peek, but didn't notice any pitched tents.

The two were fucking so vigorously that the pleather couch banged against the wall. From the looks of the couch, it wasn't its first time. If their fucking had been music, it would have been a drum solo. I wanted to suggest they try it "slow and low," but Joe had other ideas. He had Johnny take one of the bottles of water I'd procured and pump a little water into Tyla's anus before boning it.

Johnny did this, whereupon both stars realized the water was *really cold.* Tyla and Johnny soon needed a break, and Joe asked me to retrieve the lube. In the other room, the lube wasn't where I'd left it. I was the official lube girl, we were shooting an anal scene, and I'd lost the lube!

Finally I uncovered the lube, but inside, the action had recommenced. I couldn't cut in without ruining the shot so I stood outside *listening* for fifteen minutes before Joe called "cut."

When I returned, the two engaged in a piledrive position, which is not unlike the pro-wrestling move, sans neon leotards. I wondered how close Johnny was to shooting his load and what kind of range his comeshot might have. Would I get hit? Yet every time it seemed he might come they switched positions for the camera.

This went on for hours. Checking my watch, I realized I had a show to do in half an hour. Sadly, I excused myself before the finale.

Joe invited me to the next shoot two days later, which was for *The Screw Movie*, to be shot at the *Screw Magazine* offices. Joe described *The Screw Movie* as being much wackier than other porn, like the porn equivalent of the Monkees' *Head.*

The *Screw* offices are the New York equivalent of the Playboy mansion. When I arrived, I met Heather Pink, the scene's starlet. She opened her suitcase full of clothes.

"I like that polka-dotted thing," I observed.

"Oh, that's a bikini I bought in Miami when I was drunk."

"It's got a belt like Ursula Andress's bikini in *Dr. No*. I love it, but it wouldn't make sense that you're wearing a bikini indoors."

"It's a porn. It doesn't have to make sense," Heather said.

"You choose the outfit, Jen," Joe said.

"Really? Then totally, the bikini!"

"I'm really pale," Heather said.

"That's good. It's natural."

I don't know who decided all porn actors must be the same shade of orange as Oompa Loompas.

Kenny, Heather's costar, arrived, whereupon Joe explained his role to him.

"Keith is playing the *Screw* editor. You walk into his office and you're pissed because Heather is getting more publicity than you. You slam the magazine down on his desk. 'Something is going on here!' you say. Just then, Heather pokes her head up, and it's revealed that she's been giving Keith a blowjob! That's when we insert the laugh track. It's the first of many sight gags."

Joe suggested we get a shot of everyone hanging in the office. I suggested we get a shot of everyone *go-go dancing* in the office.

"Perfect!" he exclaimed. He panned from the wacky blow-job scene to the office, where the crew danced like virginal teens on *Hullabaloo*. I did "the swim" atop a desk.

After a few takes Joe called cut, and it was time to shoot Kenny and Heather doing it on a leopard-print blanket in the hallway.

"Joe, I know it's my one duty and I failed the last time, but where's the lube? I'll make sure I don't lose it."

"Heather doesn't need it. She's very wet. She'll drown us all."

"We should cut to a shot of the crew wearing emergency ponchos like we're at a Gallagher show," I suggested.

Moments later Heather and Kenny stripped naked and boned. From the sound of things, Joe hadn't lied about Heather not needing lube. I leaned in close to the action, but jumped back as she squirted clear liquid from her vagina.

After the two engaged in vaginal intercourse from every conceivable angle, they took a break. During the break, we noticed our antics in the *Screw* office had caught the attention of a neighboring office with large windows. The neighbors pointed and waved until Kenny traipsed through with his sausage dangling about, and they grew shy.

I sat down with Heather and asked her if porn ever got exhausting. "Yeah, after about three hours," she told me. Watching porn happen in real time, I realized how much work it is. Through the magic of editing, viewers are spared the anal douching and lube. It's like watching *Star Trek* and forgetting that Spock spent three hours in makeup.

Maybe my tiny contributions only made a ripple in the film's aesthetic, but I'm proud of my work. In fact, Joe was so impressed by my enthusiasm that he invited me back to work on *The Screw Movie*—just not as the lube girl.

21 THE KEY PARTY

ONE MORNING ADA from Nerve sent me an email:

I watched The Ice Storm this weekend and think you should throw a key party like the one in the movie.

Because I'd never seen *The Ice Storm*, I had no idea what a key party was. I thought maybe she was talking about *lock-and-key* parties, the British speed-dating phenomenon in which men try to match their keys to women's locks.

I Googled "key party" and discovered that it was something much different: long ago, in a magical time called the 1970s, people threw *key parties*. At these sordid, drunken soirees, male guests threw their keys into a pot, and the female guests picked a set at random, pairing up with the owner of the keys. Debauchery followed.

I called Ada. "I'm not sure this is going to work," I said. "I might alienate my friends with this one." My friends aren't swingers. Some were even in monogamous relationships. It was bad enough I'd asked them to endure my stripping debut and *Sex and the City* marathon; I was afraid asking them to swing was crossing the line.

"Just throw it and see what happens," Ada said. "And Michael thinks it's imperative you dress like Sigourney Weaver."

Reluctantly, I typed an Evite explaining the key party concept. I asked guests to choose an appropriate pseudonym and to dress in something reminiscent of '70s swingers. In conclusion, I promised copious amounts of booze. My friends aren't swingers, but they *are* drunks.

Expecting horrified responses, I sent the Evite to an assortment of friends. To my surprise, they were thrilled with the concept—not so much the swinging, but the dressing up in ridiculous outfits.

For research purposes, I watched *The Ice Storm*, a film set in 1973 suburban Connecticut. It involves two well-to-do families whose lives unravel as one husband (Kevin Kline) carries on an affair with someone else's wife (Sigourney Weaver). The shit hits the fan when both married couples attend a key party at a fabulous suburban home. When Kline tries to rig the key ceremony, he is snubbed by Sigourney, who picks another man's keys. Meanwhile, an ice storm covers Connecticut and a horrible death ensues.

Overall, not exactly an advertisement for key parties. Still, I was inspired by the '70s fashions and décor.

There were some obstacles. For starters, I don't live in a fancy New Canaan home, but rather a six-floor walkup tenement on the Lower East Side where the bathtub is in a closet in my kitchen. There is barely space for my roommate, JJ, and me, let alone a bunch of partygoers.

My friend Jennifer called and offered to help make the appetizers, since her mother was a caterer in the early '70s. The night before the party we hit Key Food. (A cheese ball needs twenty-four hours for the flavor to sink in.)

"We've got to get Chex cereal for the Chex Mix," Jennifer noted.

"It's 2006. We can *buy* Chex Mix," I said.

"Trust me," she said confidently, "it's nowhere near as good." (Later I did a taste test—she's right.)

We whizzed past the gourmet cheese aisle. "Those cheeses are *way* too highbrow," I observed. "We need Velveeta."

Loading our baskets with supplies, we wandered into the beer aisle where we found Schlitz *and* Genesee Cream Ale.

"They still make this stuff?" Jennifer gasped, holding up the Schlitz like we'd uncovered the skull of a Neanderthal man.

"Maybe it's been here since the '70s."

We grabbed what we could carry and checked out.

At home I molded the cheese ball like it was dough and became nauseated. Jennifer shredded the parsley, which I then rolled the cheese ball in. Luckily I had Palmolive and was able to soak in it afterward. Cheese ball and Chex Mix complete, Jennifer left and I spent several hours compiling a "key party playlist" containing disco greats like the Bee Gees and KC & the Sunshine Band along with classier artists like Burt Bacharach.

The next morning I popped out of bed at 8 AM, giddy with anticipation. Initially I'd been dreading the party, but now I felt that anything could happen. As I began my pre-party errands, déjà vu overwhelmed me. I was flooded with memories of being a child in the '70s, seeing several neighbors passed out on a pile of coats on my parents' bed after a wild party.

The first stop was the liquor store, where I picked up Blue Nun and Gordon's.

Considering my crib already has a groovy aesthetic, decorating was easy. If it weren't for my George Foreman Grill and iBook, guests would think it was actually 1973. However, I did make a sign that said "Keys" in red marker with flames rising off the letters. I taped it to a large Tupperware bowl. This I placed at the entrance alongside a pile of "Hello My Name Is" stickers and a Sharpie. I then created another sign that announced, "Hot Tub Inside," and taped it to the door to the bathtub in the kitchen.

"Maybe people can blow through straws to make it more like a hot tub," Tom suggested.

At 8 PM, I changed into a Sigourney Weaver-esque black halter pantsuit and requisite wooden beads. Popping open a can of Schlitz, I awaited the first swinger.

Droves of art stars arrived wearing elaborate '70s gear. They adopted wacky swinger personalities along with pseud-onyms, which they wore on the "Hello My Name Is" stick-ers. Tanya took the name "Carol," Natalie was "Bambi," Tom was "Spencer," Claudia was "Ginger," Kat was "Ursula," and Margaret was "Debbi" (dotted with a heart). Other names chosen were Lee, Donna, Alice, Trip, Sal, Burt, Reagan, B.B., Laverne, Bud, Dee-Dee, Barry, Banacek, Maurice, and Juniper, among others. I chose Janey—another nod to Sigourney Weaver's *Ice Storm* character.

The costumes and fake names had a transformative effect. Suddenly we *were* these people. Everyone called each other by their fake name. No one talked about work, Bush, or Cheney. Instead, conversation focused on astrology and par-tying. It was as if we'd time traveled.

"Who's ready to party?" Carol rhetorically asked the crowd. Everyone cheered.

"How are the kids, Debbie?" Spencer inquired.

"You know, not growin' up fast enough."

None of us actually had kids.

I served the first pitcher of Singapore Slings. Guests noted they were strong as hell.

For an hour, my buzzer rang repeatedly until my apartment was packed.

A bowl of Chex Mix was knocked over. The first of many glasses was broken. A dude in aviator shades reclined in my bathtub. A couple made out in the corner. A dance party got down in my bedroom. Ginger waltzed by in a bra with my copy of *Concerning the Spiritual in Art* stuffed down the back of her pants.

Debbie and Reagan stood in my bedroom playing "the mirror game," looking at and mirroring each other, but not touching. Meanwhile, Sal had decided it was a shame that no one could see his new bright blue Speedo-style underwear. After a few drinks, he took off his pants.

But the true lunacy began when Erin and Orion arrived and adopted the very un-groovy pseudonyms "Cancer" and "Clunt." They'd been there for less than twenty minutes when a guest exclaimed, "Uh oh, Cancer and Clunt are getting in the hot tub!"

I found Cancer completely naked and Clunt in a fetching red panty-and-bra ensemble. I poured bubble bath in the running water.

"Get in!" they urged.

Banacek, who was standing nearby, stripped down to his Calvin Klein briefs and hopped in. Inspired, I ran into my bedroom and changed into a *Charlie's Angels*–style bathing suit.

Clunt, Cancer, Banacek, and I lounged in the hot tub while chatting with the crowd in the kitchen. Others wanted to hang in the hot tub, so Banacek and I went to my room, where we toweled off. Several people milled about while Sal reclined on top of a pile of coats on my bed, wearing his Speedo underwear, a white T-shirt, and a red sweatshirt.

He looked like a member of the 1976 Olympic swim team. Banacek and I lay down next to him, where we were joined by Dee-Dee, the resident hippie chick.

The debauched spirit of the '70s hung in the air like a heavy dose of Enjoli. Sal and I began kissing as Dee-Dee and Banacek made out. Wig-clad partygoers hovered over us watching.

Straddling Sal, I ran my hands over his body. Our retro swimsuits pressed together like a pornographic American Apparel ad. Dee-Dee removed Banacek's "swimsuit" while I slid Sal's Speedo down his thighs. In the background the Brothers Gibb cooed, "Nobody gets too much love anymore," as Dee-Dee and I did our best to prove them wrong, performing simultaneous fellatio upon the delighted recipients. Banacek pulled off Dee-Dee's panties and began licking her while I used my free hand to pleasure Banacek, who in turn licked me while Sal and Banacek took turns kissing Dee-Dee and me.

By way of the key party experiment, I'd discovered a greater pastime: the four-way! However, the fun was quickly interrupted when half-a-dozen people wandered into the room. Dee-Dee couldn't find her underwear, which Banacek had flung halfway across the room. A small panty search party was formed while I changed out of my bathing suit and into a mini-dress sans panties. The atmosphere of liberation moved me to go commando.

In the kitchen, the gathering had devolved into pure madness. An unidentified guest had just eaten a Cheeto out of Cancer's foreskin. People danced and made out and every few minutes someone turned out the lights. The sound of things crashing and breaking mingled with sweet disco sounds. Dee-Dee moved on from Banacek and was dancing closely with a hippie dude no one knew.

The madness went on for hours and was so rockin' no one wanted to leave, even for sex. The key drawing didn't occur until approximately 3 AM. It would have happened at two-thirty, but I couldn't find the keys. I lose my own keys on a daily basis; I don't know what made me think I could be responsible for other peoples'. When I finally found them, Barry, that crazy prankster, had linked all of the keys together, forming one giant key. In my inebriated state it took a good fifteen minutes to separate them.

Because almost no one in New York drives and because subway Metrocards look exactly alike, guests had put *apartment* keys rather than vehicle keys in the pot. I noticed there were straight, gay, and bisexual guests hovering over the bowl. It wasn't as simple as *The Ice Storm*, where everyone was straight and married. How would this ever work out?

Yvonne, a gorgeous bisexual woman, went first and chose Clunt, a lesbian. Success! Everyone cheered. Dennis, a straight dude, reached in and chose Cancer, a bisexual man. Not so appropriate. The two made out anyway. Up next, Dee-Dee plunged her hand into the pot and chose the unidentified hippie's keys. They gave each other a knowing glance and it became clear they'd cheated. They happily left for a pre-arranged tryst in Brooklyn. Sticking my hand in, I realized I probably couldn't leave with anyone because people were passed out all over my apartment. I chose Bambi and Bud's keys. Sadly, I handed them back to the blond, bubbly Bambi, and she promised me a "rain check—anytime." A few other guests drew keys that were grossly inappropriate before leaving for the night.

The next morning, amazingly, I awoke without a hangover,

probably because I was still drunk. I lay in bed talking to Burt, who had driven into the city and had to stay over.

"There are gonna be a lot of locked-out people this morning. There are still a lot of keys in that bowl," he noted.

"Yeah, I didn't organize it too well. And the kitchen is trashed out there. I keep thinking my parents are gonna come home from vacation and discover the mess. Then I remember it's okay."

Fearfully, we wandered into the kitchen. Chex Mix and broken glass crunched under our shoes. The full-length mirror was shattered.

"Seven years of bad luck," I observed.

"Yeah," he said, "it was bad luck when I almost sliced my neck open on it."

I said goodbye to Burt and commenced cleaning, whereupon I discovered the full extent of the night's debauchery. A pair of men's underpants lay next to my bed along with a woman's shirt that wasn't mine. Cig butts, beer cans, and spilled food were everywhere. Opening the bathtub door, I found an undressed troll, a cherry stem, several cans of beer, and *Concerning the Spiritual in Art* sitting in what had been the make-believe hot tub.

Still, it was worth it for the Kodak moments and masturbatory fodder. Many guests declared that it was the craziest party they'd ever attended. As Dee-Dee later pointed out, "The theme of sexual liberation colored everything."

True. I'm not so sure I would have been as quick to drop to my knees in a Bee Gees–serenaded four-way had it not been for the wild atmosphere. It had been a collective game of roleplay that freed us from judgment because we were only pretending. And I'm guessing that's exactly why married couples did it in the '70s

22 SAVED

AFTER THE KEY party, people constantly asked me when I was going to throw my next party. It made me feel like a poor version of the Great Gatsby.

Privately, I wondered if my life was becoming a bit too much like Gatsby's—totally out of control. But any thoughts of reining it in were aborted when Malcolm announced that he was coming to town.

While I had only exchanged two letters with Anthony, Malcolm and I had stayed in touch, maybe because Malcolm knew what the internet was.

The record he'd cut with the "A&R geezers" had done well, and I fretted that I was now just one in a legion of groupies. But like Sandy and Danny reunited at Rydell High, our summer lovin' continued unabated when he arrived. And he was even wilder than I remembered. One night we went into a store to buy a six-pack and came out carrying a keg.

By our last night together, my internal organs ached.

"Thank God you live in another country. I don't think my

liver could take it otherwise," I told him.

"Yeah, we would destroy each other."

"You're a bad influence, but I'm going to miss you."

"I wanna be a teetotaler when I get back, but it's impossible with the band."

"Same thing with performing. But you can never quit the band and I can never quit doing what I do because we *can't* do anything else."

"I keep hoping I'm gonna find someone to calm me down. *I want someone to save me.*"

"I used to want someone to save me. Then I realized every dude I found wanted *me* to save *him*. Everyone is broken and I've given up."

"I think it's sad that you've given up."

"I think it's sad that you're still trying."

Malcolm left the next morning, and as I walked to the drugstore to buy Visine for my terribly bloodshot eyes, a born-again handed me a pamphlet. Normally Holy Rollers stare at me like I'm beyond redemption, so I must've really looked like shit.

"What's your destination?" the pamphlet asked in bold letters, which I think meant, "Are you going to heaven or hell?"

As I exited the store, the born-again leapt in front of me.

"Have you been saved?" she demanded.

"No. I've given up."

The following day, I got an email from Malcolm:

Had really good fun an was really nice to see ya. As soon as I've saved myself I'll return to save u.

23 GROUPIE

IT APPEARED I had entered a phase of exclusively boning musicians. I thought about how to bankroll this predilection into a paycheck and suggested to Ada that I write a groupie piece.

I'd been a groupie in the making all my life. When I was fourteen, I snagged a copy of *Hammer of the Gods* off my mother's nightstand. What should have served as a cautionary tale of the dangers of one-night stands became my favorite masturbatory fodder. Soon, the crumpled book automatically opened to a photo of Jimmy Page seductively stroking his double-neck guitar. Dreams of running away from Maryland to pursue a super-groupie lifestyle danced in my head.

But the popular music of my teens was a far cry from Zeppelin. Video killed the radio star, and I was left with Chicago, Milli Vanilli, and Paula Abdul. There *were* groupies in the late '80s, but they followed bands like Poison. Since I refuse to bone a man who uses more hair products than I do, I opted for college instead.

Yet my fantasy of making sweet love to a rock star never died.

This could have been one of the reasons I was attracted to Malcolm. Maybe he was the manifestation of my teenage yearnings. But my relationship with him was too complicated to masquerade as one of my "labs." I wanted to be honest with readers, to begin with a hypothesis and work up to a conclusion. I would have to start from scratch.

I began with research—a rereading of *Hammer of the Gods* and a careful study of *I'm with the Band*. Coincidentally, Pamela Des Barres was reading that night at a bar in Brooklyn. "My God," I whispered to Tom as we eyed Pamela across bar. "She slept with Mick Jagger, Jimmy Page, and Keith Moon. I feel like I'm about to meet a Nobel Prize winner."

During the Q&A, I asked, "If one wanted to sleep with a rock star in this day and age, how would one go about it?"

Pamela responded that it helps if you're in a profession that gives you access to rock stars, be it modeling, acting, or journalism. *Awesome*, I thought. *I'm a journalist*. Problem is, I was writing about sex, not music. Most musicians would run from me rather than have their fetishes or penis size revealed. Maybe I could masquerade as a *Tiger Beat* writer.

After the reading, I watched *Almost Famous* (a coming-of-age story about a teenage rock journalist in the '70s, featuring Kate Hudson as a groupie with a heart of gold) and learned that unless your beloved rock star has given you an engagement ring, you run the risk of being sold for fifty bucks and a case of beer at any time.

My research complete, it was time to select a band. This proved difficult. Bands today just don't party like they used to. It's hard to imagine Death Cab for Cutie inserting a mudshark into anyone's vag.

My friend Dave suggested the Rolling Stones, who were playing a benefit concert at Radio City Music Hall that week. "Or," he pointed out, "you could be a groupie for the billionaires who bought tickets."

The Stones seemed a little ambitious, seeing as how they're the most famous rock band on earth. First I would try cutting my chops on a smaller act.

I turned to MySpace, a groupie's paradise. Not only can you troll through thousands of bands, you can send them messages. But after finding too many bands that listed the Dave Matthews Band and Blink-182 among their influences, I retreated in horror.

Frustrated, I called Tom, whose friend Chris runs Matador Records. "Would it be too weird if you asked Chris to help me find a band?"

Tom phoned Chris and called me back. "He's got the perfect band, but you have to act fast because they're playing tonight." Early Man, a metal outfit from Ohio, was playing at North Six in Brooklyn along with two other metal bands, Priestess and The Sword.

Because groupies travel in packs or pairs, I called my friend Dodge (short for Margaret Dodge, which we changed because Margaret isn't a good groupie name). Hesitantly, she agreed to join me. Tom also decided to go, on the off chance that Priestess was an all-girl group.

Quickly, I threw together a getup. Mirroring the styles in *Almost Famous*, I chose a vintage lace mini-dress, purple tights, and white ankle boots. After covering the bags under my eyes with concealer, I made fake bags using kohl eyeliner.

We arrived just in time to witness a strapping bouncer escort an unruly metalhead out to the street. The Sword had just taken the stage. They were so deafening we could hear them from outside the club.

"It's gonna be really loud," said Dodge, shuddering.

"You got an extra ticket?" a stoned-looking, pentagram-accessorized youth asked her.

Chris and his wife met us and suggested we get a pre-show drink. On our way to a nearby bar, we ran into Mike, Early Man's vocalist, and Vince, the drummer for Priestess. They both had flowing brown hair and skinny legs that fit nicely into their weathered jeans. Chris introduced us but didn't mention my ulterior motive of hot rock star lovin'.

"Oh my GOD!" Dodge exclaimed as they walked off. "Vince is so hot. I get dibs."

Placing dibs on the object of your affection is part of the groupie code of honor. From the moment Dodge chose Vince, I would not go near him.

A few drinks later we returned to the club. Priestess had just taken the stage. Tom was disappointed there wasn't a single chick in the band, but we were amazed at how hard they rocked. Vince thrashed his see-through drum kit like a madman.

"I can't see his face," Dodge complained.

"I can't see any of their faces," I said. "There's so much hair. I'm not sure they have faces."

We rushed to the foot of the stage to get a better look and were instantaneously swept up in the madness. Legions of dudes banged their heads, genuflecting with devil horns. I too raised my horns in the air until Dodge pointed out that I was actually making the "hang loose" sign.

The music made me forget that I was on assignment. I was a groupie, completely in love with the sound and the longhaired, beautiful dudes making it—two guitars, drums, and a bass playing fast, hard, and loud.

"Priestess rules the world!" Dodge screamed.

Despite our desperate shrieks for an encore, their set came to an end forty-five minutes later. We had to maul Priestess immediately. Finding Tom and Chris, I begged them to help us get backstage. While Chris explained to Tom that he couldn't do all the work for me, I noticed that the guy manning the velvet rope to the backstage area appeared to be staring into space.

Grabbing Dodge's hand, we slipped past him and giggled uncontrollably as we made our way to the downstairs greenroom where we found Priestess hanging out. We introduced ourselves and someone offered me a Budweiser. I was in heaven.

The members of Priestess—Mikey, Mike, Dan, and Vince—hailed from Montreal. They were nice, gracious, smart, and funny—traits the general public might not associate with metal bands.

While Dodge attempted to engage Vince in a discussion about methods for replacing liquids after a show, I ran back upstairs to tell Tom triumphantly where we were.

Tom and I returned to the greenroom and chatted with the quartet for as long as possible. Even when the headliners, Early Man, went on, we remained, not wanting to miss a moment of backstage glory. But a word of caution to would-be groupies: Never go beer for beer with a metal band, especially a Canadian metal band.

We were still drinking with Priestess when Early Man

returned. A member of the band took off his shirt and wrung out the sweat.

"I feel honored to have witnessed that," said Dodge. When Priestess was out of the room for a second, Dodge buried her face in Vince's jacket. "I never knew a metalhead could smell so good," she gushed.

Priestess, Early Man, and Chris invited us along to the Turkey's Nest, a Brooklyn dive bar. Dodge opted out after realizing she was too drunk.

Once there, I tried to impress Mike, Priestess's bassist, by ordering a drink in Elvish. The bartender served us thirty-two-ounce Styrofoam cups filled with Budweiser. Though I was drunk and confused, I managed to chat up Mike for hours until we were the only people left in the bar. I think I even offered him an off-the-record quickie, which he politely refused because of "a girlfriend in Canada."

Even so, I was delighted to hang with the bassist of my new favorite band. My excitement was quashed only when the bartender hovered over us and said, "We're closed. You really have to leave."

Mike walked me to a cab and said goodbye before sauntering off to the Priestess RV, which I can only dream about (or masturbate to).

The following day, Dodge and I exchanged a flurry of emails regarding our rapid descent into metal fandom. But while Dodge studied the Priestess tour schedule, I had work to do. Though I'd failed with Priestess, the Stones concert was only a couple days away.

Kat agreed to go with me, despite what she was convinced would be "certain failure." But even if I had to prop Keith up and give him mouth-to-mouth, I was determined to succeed. (Remembering the code of honor, I'd placed dibs on Keith.)

We arrived at Radio City an hour before the show. The place was swarming with security. Circling the block, we found a gaggle of dudes in laminated crew necklaces hanging out next to a large golden door labeled "Stage Entrance." We stood next to them.

Because tickets to the show cost between $300 and $1,000, even the audience members were arriving in limos, making it tough to determine which vehicle was carrying the rock gods. Many of the concertgoers were wearing business suits. I was offended.

"You'd think these dudes would have the decency to remove their ties," I noted. "Why don't we just try to get in and then act like we didn't know we needed tickets?"

Turning to one of the crew, I asked, "What do you think the chances of us gaining entrance sans a ticket are?"

"Not so good," he answered. "There's the Radio City security, the Stones' security, and the NYPD."

The fact that the temperature had dipped into the thirties could explain why Kat, two eBay autograph hunters, and I were the only fans waiting outside. Our eyes shifted between the arriving cars and the stage entrance. "I don't think they'd be so obvious as to arrive in a fancy limo," I said. "I bet they're gonna pull up in a DHL truck."

A silver fox waved a Mercedes limo into a reserved spot. "That guy is wearing a mock turtleneck. He is definitely someone," Kat observed. "A celebrity must be in that car."

"Yeah, and I think Keith is driving," I said after the Mercedes swerved and almost ran down the turtleneck-clad fox.

Suddenly an Enterprise rental van emerged. The crew

opened the back and began to pull something out. "Maybe they're wheeling them out on gurneys."

We watched the back of the Enterprise van for over an hour before my face started freezing.

One of the autograph hunters got word that the Stones had gone in on the other side. "We had to choose the wrong side," Kat sighed.

Disappointed, cold, and hungry, we went off in search of sustenance and warmth. We would return after their set and try to catch them on their *way out*.

We found a place called Ellen's Stardust Diner. A sign on the door advertised *singing waiters*.

Inside, a maître d' whisked us to a table in the front row.

"We're total VIP's," Kat enthused, checking out the crooning waiter before us. "Is he singing George Michael?"

"I believe he is," I said. "I have a sneaking suspicion he *might not be* straight."

He exited the stage and took our order, whereupon another singing waiter took his place, belting out Billy Joel's "You May Be Right." Stealthily, he jumped onto the chair behind Kat and shook his ass inches from her head.

"Woohoo!" I shouted, making devil horns. A table of fanny-pack-clad tourist women eyed us suspiciously. "If I were wearing a bra, I'd throw it at him."

"If bras weren't so expensive, I'd throw mine," said Kat.

A singing waitress followed. "Who likes show tunes?" she asked the crowd, which responded with dead silence. "Or do you guys like rock 'n' roll?"

"Rock 'n' roll!" Kat shouted.

"'Free Bird!'" I added.

She belted out a Tina Turner tune and exited the stage.

A lanky redheaded waiter began singing, "What's New, Pussycat?" while expertly gyrating his hips like Tom Jones.

"He's hot," I said. "I wonder when he gets off work." It wasn't hard to catch his eye considering we were the only people watching. I winked and blew him a kiss. He winked back at me.

His song finished and he recommenced carrying trays of cheese fries and hot dogs. "That's not right. He's a star," I cried.

Just then the tip jar came around. Taking out a flyer with my picture on it, I jotted down my email address and slipped it in along with a couple bucks. Satisfied that I'd succeeded in making some headway as a singing-waiter groupie, we finished our snack and headed back to Radio City.

The Stones were still onstage. We pressed our ears to the golden door and listened. It was almost like being at the show.

They played eight more songs before the music stopped and the audience began filtering out. Barricades were brought out. Security asked us and about ten other fans to stand behind them.

"When do you think they're gonna come out?" Kat asked.

"They have to climb inside their life-regeneration tanks first."

We waited along with the other fans for close to an hour, at which point the barricades were removed and Kat and I realized they'd already gone. I don't know if the Stones don magic invisibility suits when entering and exiting arenas, but we never even caught a glimpse of them.

Exhausted and cold, we called it a night.

When the Stones sang, "You Can't Always Get What You Want," they could have been talking about this experiment. I'd lacked the patience and sneakiness needed to get in the pants of the objects of my adulation. About the only sneaky thing we'd done was molest Vince's clothing.

Still, when I looked up "groupie" in the dictionary, one definition was "any enthusiastic fan or supporter." In that sense, I'd succeeded.

And Dodge was converted: "Now I *am* a groupie," she said. Though she pointed out that she'd felt a little like an uncool aunt while hanging in the greenroom. "Instead of asking Vince about fluid replacement, I should have been more concerned about how he was going to get rid of certain other fluids."

24 COUGAR HUNT

MICHAEL FROM NERVE read an article in the *New York Post* about older women, sometimes referred to as "cougars," who prowl the urban jungle in search of boy toys. Inspired, he suggested I get out there and bone some barely legal men for science.

"Just make sure you check their ID before you sleep with them," he said.

Lately, I'd screwed *nothing but* younger men. I wondered what would make this experiment different from every other day of my life—maybe the act of actually *trying*.

A funny thing happened when I turned thirty: men my own age wanted nothing to do with me, while younger men suddenly hit on me left and right.

I told my friends about the assignment.

"Why would a woman want to sleep with a nineteen-year-old?" asked my friend Lori. "You'll only end up getting your vagina mishandled. Trust me."

My friend Dave was more encouraging. "When I was

twenty-three," he shared, "I moved in with an actress who was forty-two. It was absolutely wonderful. We both knew it wasn't forever. She had a lot to teach me, and I was eager to learn. And I could learn again and again—many times a night."

Turning to the web for guidance, I found several sites offering tips on hunting actual mountain lions, featuring pictures of hunters guffawing at the camera with dead cougars draped over their shoulders. Once I finished sobbing, I found urbancougar.com. It describes "a sophisticated species of female who seeks the pleasure of younger males."

"Sophisticated?" Bruce asked, after checking out the site. "They sell 'Liquor? I don't even know her' T-shirts."

"And beer koozies."

Though not the classiest site on the web, urbancougar offered articles, an open letter to Heather Locklear (encouragement from willing prey), cougar classifications, and a handy list of hunting tips. *Don't be afraid to slum it* the site suggested. Young men like cheap beer. Where there is cheap beer, there are young men. The site also encouraged cougars to *keep it light*. "Because nothing scares off prey faster than reality."

As for where to find young playthings, I consulted my friend Johnny, a twenty-one-year-old film school dropout.

"Dallas BBQ has a really good happy hour, and they're not too strict about asking for ID, so a lot of students go there." He also suggested "anywhere cheap near NYU."

Though real cougars hunt alone, urban cougars travel in packs, so I invited a posse of wildcats along for the hunt: "Red Alert," a forty-five-year-old divorced, redheaded, Latina performer with the body of a twenty-seven-year-old (whose real name is Michelle), and Jennifer, who'd helped make the giant cheese ball for my key party. Though she's married, she offered to go along for the Kodak moments. Tanya, at twenty-six, was a C.I.T. (Cougar in Training). And at thirty-three, I fell into the "puma" category (a cougar under forty).

Operation Mrs. Robinson got under way at my apartment, where Red, Jennifer, and I conferred over a six-pack of Rolling Rock while getting gussied up. Jennifer applied dark red lipstick, while Red powdered her nose, leaving her zit uncovered to appear younger.

"That's the only benefit of adult acne," she pointed out.

"I'm so tired of the double standard," I said, pulling on a black mini and leopard-print halter. "When I mentioned this expedition to certain dudes, they acted as if I were opening another Neverland Ranch. Meanwhile, half of them won't even look at a woman over thirty."

"I actually don't think men in their forties are that different from men in their twenties," Red pointed out. "The main difference is that when a man is in his forties, his back hair starts to connect with his chest hair."

"It becomes like a shirt," Jennifer added. "Also," she said, "their balls change over the years."

"It would be cool to do time-lapse recordings of nutsacks."

Moving off the subject of aging, we brainstormed pickup lines.

Jennifer suggested, "My biological clock is ticking, but it looks like you're right on schedule."

And Red came up with, "I've been giving blowjobs since before you were born."

We started our hunt at BBQ, where the host tried to seat us in the basement, away from all the young people.

"No way!" Red exclaimed. "We wanna be where the action is."

"They tried to put us in the basement because we're old," I moaned, once we were finally seated upstairs.

Jennifer and I split a pitcher of light beer and Red got a Blue Hawaiian that came in a glass the size of a goldfish bowl. Throwing caution to the wind, we also ordered a small onion loaf.

Tanya arrived wearing a strategically torn "MILF" T-shirt. Her hair was in an updo worthy of *Passions* and her lips were lined with pencil two shades darker than her neutral lipstick. Next to us, a table of young women pointed to her and laughed.

"I see the twins are out," she said, noting Jennifer's excessive cleavage. "Oh, by the way, guys, tonight I'm 'Tanya Fox.' I work as an agent's assistant and have a six-year-old kid."

"Maybe I should have a fake persona. Do you guys think young men will find me sexier if they think I'm divorced?" I asked.

"Yeah," Jennifer answered. "Then you can use the pickup line, 'You remind me of my fourth husband.'"

"There's not much prey here," I observed.

"Everyone looks like they're on dates," Red noted, picking at the onion loaf. "This is gross."

"I know," I said. "It's like the scrapings off a George Foreman grill. Let's finish our drinks and get the hell out."

We paid for our drinks and the waitress brought us fresh-naps for wiping the grease from our fingers. Tanya suggested I go up to dudes, wipe their faces with the fresh-naps, and say, "You look dirty."

Leaving BBQ, we walked past NYU's Weinstein Hall,

where I asked a group of students where we could meet college men.

They directed us to Josie Wood's, a nearby pub where Tanya and Red ordered apple martinis and Jen and I ordered beer. The place wasn't as hopping as we'd hoped. In fact, it was full of dudes *sitting down* with other women. The women glared at us with contempt. Our ridiculous outfits conveyed one thing: we were on the prowl.

"Excuse me," I stopped our waitress. "We're trying to meet college boys. Do you know where they hang out?"

She spoke with a heavy accent. "You want young guy you have to come here another time. This place is usually packed. But tonight it dead. Usually it full of young guys. You won't find any white-hairs here."

"White-hairs," I noted. "She said it like it was a disease."

Tanya and Red finished their martinis and filled their empty glasses with some of our beer, creating a new cocktail, "the pee-tini."

On our way out, we witnessed a hot older woman entering the bar with a much younger man.

"Mrrrrrrrow!" Red whispered. "There goes a cougar."

The younger man overheard her and snapped, "What did you say about my lady?"

"There goes a cute one," Red stammered, avoiding a barroom brawl.

We left Josie Wood's and headed for Grassroots Tavern on St. Mark's Place, where I hung out back when I was barely legal. Upon entering, we were pleased to find the place swarming with young bucks. Hipsters in freshly pressed Led Zeppelin T-shirts mingled with women who wore jeans and no makeup. We stood out like sore thumbs in our slutty outfits. Undeterred, we zoned in on a smattering of hotties who were sitting at a table with a woman their own age.

"Don't worry. We'll get rid of her," I said.

Red made the first move, approaching our prey with her digital camera.

"Would you mind taking a picture of me and my friends?" she asked.

"Not at all."

We made crazy cougar faces and growled at the camera, attracting the attention of everyone at the bar. The photos look alarmingly like the "cougar sighting" photos on urban-cougar.com.

"What's your name?" I asked our photographer, who had a long black mane and barely-there facial hair.

"Corey."

"You mean like Corey Haim and Corey Feldman?"

"Yes."

"That is awesome. Do you have a girlfriend?"

"Yeah."

"Damn. I'm trying to get with a younger man."

"You should talk to my friend Dustin. He's twenty-two and he's a virgin."

"No way. You're making that up. I don't believe that his name is Dustin or that he's a virgin."

"I swear. Ask him."

"We should pull an *Almost Famous*–style deflowering on him," Red suggested.

Dustin was sitting in the corner wearing a corduroy blazer, a T-shirt, and jeans. His longish hair hung over his eyes as he hunched over his beer. Like Dustin Hoffman in *The Graduate*, he appeared disillusioned and confused. The night wasn't getting any younger and neither was he, so I sidled up to him and asked him point blank if he'd like his virgin cherry popped by an experienced sex columnist. He insisted that he was not a virgin and kindly rejected me on the basis that he and Corey were moving to Arkansas in the morning.

"I really just want to hang out with my friends tonight," he said. "I'm not going to see them again for a long time."

"Have any of your *friends* ever been to fellatio school?" I asked him.

Dustin turned three shades of red and shifted around nervously, which for some reason made me moist. I felt like Mrs. Robinson asking Benjamin Braddock to unzip her dress.

He suggested we talk in the back of the bar, probably because he was embarrassed to be seen with me. In the back room we chatted and pressed together so closely he left corduroy imprints on my chest. Were Grassroots Tavern's bathrooms not disgusting, I would have suggested we sneak into a stall and get it on.

Tanya interrupted to announce she was leaving. Jennifer and Red had grown bored with Grassroots and insisted we move on.

We planted a flurry of kisses onto Dustin's blushing cheeks before heading for our next destination, where we took the "don't be afraid to slum it" tip to heart. Mars Bar is *the* vilest bar in New York City, maybe the world. The awning outside reads "Day Care for Drunks," and you can actually smell the bar from the sidewalk. At Mars Bar, I have seen (among other things) a man crash his head through the window so he could finish an argument with a prostitute, a man pass out on my shoe, and a man scream the word "cocksucker" at the top of his lungs for over an hour. In recent years, Mars Bar has become popular with college kids and young punk rockers who go there for the cheap drinks and ambience.

By the time we got there, it was past midnight. Though we were starting to feel old, embarrassed, and unsuccessful, we were emboldened by alcohol and the notion that we had nothing left to lose.

A redheaded bartender who wore a retro outfit reminiscent of The Who at their most foppish took our order. He looked familiar.

"Now he is hot," I whispered. "Most men can't pull off bangs."

"How old are you?" Red asked him. "You don't look old enough to be bartending."

"I'm twenty-one."

"Jailbait!" Red exclaimed as he waltzed off to get our beers.

"He's like a fresh baguette," I said. "I want to eat him."

He returned with three beers.

"I like your bangs," I said. "Are you in a band?"

"Yeah."

"That's where I know you from! The Neon something?"

"The Neon Neurotics."

"That's right. You guys rock. We met outside some bar on Rivington Street."

"Oh yeah, I remember you."

"What's your name?"

"Damien."

"Damien, are you gay?"

"No."

"Do you like older women?"

His eyes lit up. "Oh yeah, I like them until they get possessive."

"Oh. I'm horribly possessive. I'm a Leo."

Damien and I discussed star signs, music, and the perils of working at Mars Bar. He proved to be the perfect prey, since he was trapped behind the bar and couldn't run away. Meanwhile some dude who looked like he'd been drinking at Mars Bar every day since opening night was hitting on Red.

"You're so beautiful," he gushed, hovering over her like a corpse in skinny jeans. As Red evaded his cadaver-like hands, Jennifer was passing out on the bar next to me, cradling her purse like it was a stuffed animal. Afraid she might get head lice from the bar, we roused her from her slumber.

Red used the opportunity to escape the affections of the Crypt Keeper, helping Jennifer to a cab. I continued flirting with Damien, who gave me his digits.

Unlike Dustin, I got the feeling Damien had been with plenty of women, old and young. He'd probably gotten more ass than most men twice his age.

"I got his number!" I told Red when she returned.

"You mean you're not gonna wait till he gets off work and ambush him?"

"Dude, no way can I sit here till closing time. People at Mars Bar never leave at last call. He's going to be here for at least four more hours."

"Actually, I'm not sure the people here ever go home."

Still, we tried to wait it out, hoping Damien might leave early—not likely, since he was the sole bartender at the beck and call of a roomful of dangerous drunks. Eventually, Red and I were too exhausted to continue. Like a puma burying her slain prey for later, I slipped Damien's number into my pocket and threw on my jacket. I would use it another time, but for now I was no longer hungry. One of the great things about growing older is appreciating the comforts of home and knowing when to call it a night. I spent my twenties passing out in strange places and having sloppy, drunken sex wherein I often faked the big O to protect the ego of whichever dude I was boning.

At home, I climbed under the covers and passed out, exhausted from the hunt. Though I hadn't rocked the cradle, the safari alone had worn me out.

The next day I woke up with a heinous head cold. At least I'd escaped Mars Bar without a case of pubic lice. I looked and felt so awful I was glad I hadn't taken anyone home with me. No man should ever be forced to endure the sound of me coughing up phlegm at 9 AM.

My chest slathered in Vicks VapoRub, I called Red.

"So how'd you feel about the night?" I asked.

"It was a total waste of time and effort," she said. "Beauty really is in the eye of the beholder. To those young guys we were like old trolls, but to the old dude at Mars Bar, I was the most beautiful woman in the world. Plus I think you have to meet people organically. Picking up dudes in bars is humiliating."

Later, I spoke to Tanya, who agreed.

"It was mostly embarrassing," she said. "We seriously could have been 100, because that's how people reacted."

"When I was twenty-one, I used to think thirty-three-year-olds were old. Little did I realize how immature I'd be."

"I think we stabbed ourselves in the foot by actually trying."

"Yeah, if we'd just sat there and not dressed like cougars, guys probably wouldn't have run from us. We were too proactive."

"So did you get any action?"

"No. I got a phone number. It might not even be real, though. I'll have to wait till I can breathe out of my right nostril before I call him."

"Well, then it wasn't a total failure."

"I guess not. God, that onion loaf was gross. It tasted dirty."

"I think it was a metaphor for the whole evening: it looked good at first, but then after five bites you realized it was really unappetizing and grew embarrassed for just having it at your table."

READERS WERE OUTRAGED that I'd failed in both my groupie and my cougar columns, and I couldn't blame them. I'd gotten lazy and prudish. I felt I owed it to them and to me to get some twenty-one-year-old musician ass. I would do follow-up fieldwork and turn the onion loaf into lemonade.

Conveniently, Damien's band was playing at a bar one block away from my open mike. So after my show, I *casually* walked JJ by the venue while wearing candy-apple-red six-inch heels and a mod micro-mini-dress. There I found my unwitting lab partner sitting outside, catching some air with his bandmates.

"Reverend Jen!" he exclaimed, bounding to his feet.

"Did I miss your set?"

"Yeah, we just finished. We're all hanging out. You should come in."

Not wanting to subject JJ to loud rock 'n' roll, I promised to come back after dropping her off at home.

When I returned, a bartender directed me to a mysterious basement where a gaggle of hep cats were engaged in a groovy dance party. It reminded me of the beatnik den where Shirley Feeney improvised her notorious "scarf dance." Plus it was filled with barely legal men dressed in adorable mod attire. In the world of cougars, I'd just hit the jackpot.

As I roamed the territory, prey approached from all directions, attracted by the cougar scent of Chanel No. 5. Because the place was also filled with barely legal women, the attention surprised me. Maybe younger men really do like older women, and it's not just propaganda that's sprung from the union of Demi and Ashton.

Eventually I located my primary prey, who was settled into his natural habitat: a barstool. We drank Budweiser and chitchatted about music until we engaged in precoital necking. Our bodies pressed together, and the cool dampness of his shirt made me hot, the result of a "sweaty drummer" fetish I developed upon seeing Keith Moon in *The Rolling Stones Rock and Roll Circus*.

Though I couldn't wait to get him back to my lair, he insisted we first acquire refreshments. At the bodega, we purchased two forties of Budweiser, and Damien got a pack of cigs.

In my boudoir, we undressed and fondled each other while simultaneously sipping from our giant bottles of domestic beer.

"You should have called me. We could have done this a lot sooner," he said, recklessly puffing on a cig.

"Honestly I don't know where I put your number. Unless I write something down on my hand, I lose it."

"Me too."

"Maybe we should write our numbers on each other."

I handed Damien a Sharpie, and he wrote his name and number in giant letters across my thigh. He then encouraged me to write my name and number directly above his penis. Once our naked, pasty bodies were adorned with each other's digits, we got down to business—licking, sucking, and kissing each other in a frenzied manner.

Sadly, fellatio school is wasted on the young. I have a feeling that as long as I wasn't actually biting his penis off, he would have enjoyed himself. Finally we got down to boning, whereupon a benefit of the cougar/prey connection became clear: while many cougars are capable of coming several times in one night, their prey can also come several times in one night. It's as though their system is comprised of equal parts blood, sweat, Budweiser, and semen.

And one of the benefits of doing a drummer is their ability to "hit the skins" with timing and rhythm. We fucked. I came. He came. He flipped me over and we fucked again. He came again. This went on until I noticed something coming through my window: sunlight.

"Oh my God, is it morning?" I asked.

"I think so."

The clock read 6 AM.

25 THE THREE MOST BEAUTIFUL WORDS

JUST AS I was returning to my slutty habits, something phenomenal happened:

Daniel returned from Hollywood.

He was the only man I'd ever slept with who went out west and wasn't swallowed by a mysterious smog. His show had been cancelled, and the TV people left him remarkably unscathed. They hadn't cut and gelled his hair or waxed his eyebrows. I fully expected him to have shacked up with one of his perfect-looking costars, but that hadn't happened either.

According to him, I was a "classy lady"—something he hadn't found out west. Compared to fake tans, bleached hair, and silicone boobs, I suppose I did appear elegant, if you overlooked my drinking Budweiser and sleeping in a filthy SpongeBob nightgown from Kmart.

I invited him over, and we sat on my roof drinking wine. As the sun went down and the Woolworth Building cast its ethereal glow upon us, we traded the view of the skyline for the view of my bedroom ceiling.

We smoked a little pot, took off our clothes, and got in bed, where we traded caresses and oral favors until I finally climbed on top and straddled his exquisite member. I leaned back, closed my eyes, and rocked back and forth.

As I did, he whispered, "Look at me."

I would've been less shocked if he'd asked me to wear a nun's habit and fuck him with a black leather dildo. Sex for me had become like riding the subway: no eye contact. Of all the possible variations: vagina and penis or vagina and tongue or tongue and penis or sometimes penis and anus or penis and penis or even anus and tongue, this was the most intimate.

I used to think "I love you" were the three most beautiful words. But experience taught me that men who were lying, cheating, or about to break up with you said "I love you" the most. Then, for a while, I thought the three most beautiful words might be "open bar tonight," but after too many hangovers, I changed my mind.

Daniel taught me the three most beautiful words that night.

Look at me.

I opened my eyes and stared into his eyes. I liked what I saw: a real human being.

If Daniel had just been gorgeous, I might not have cared. New York is crawling with hot men, and I'd fucked my share of them. But Daniel was *nice*. He told me he loved my freckles, that my scar was sexy, my tiny boobs "perfect," and my voice like the sound of "a baby unicorn."

We began seeing each other a few times a week.

I wasn't sure what to do about my column, since it was heavily reliant on me fucking an assortment of people. Though Daniel and I hadn't discussed monogamy, I was done screwing around.

26 SEX TOY OLYMPICS

ERIN LANDED HER dream job as a sex toy reviewer for an online magazine. It was the equivalent of a raging alcoholic landing a gig as a wine critic. Despite her love of vibrators, she'd obtained more free sex toys than one vagina could handle. She offered to outsource them to me for science on the condition that she supervise. I didn't think me masturbating in front of a lesbian would bother Daniel, so I took her up on it.

I named the event the Sex Toy Olympics. It seemed appropriate, since New York had lost its bid to host the 2012 Olympic games. I would keep the Olympic dream alive by presenting an event that didn't require a billion-dollar stadium, athletic prowess, or the approval of a committee. Honoring the ancient Greek traditions of athletic nudity and phallus veneration, a cavalcade of toys would be rigorously tested on my vag.

Erin was the event's first official sponsor, my Gatorade or Coca-Cola.

We exchanged a flurry of preparatory emails and calls to ensure a smooth operation. Given the breadth of toys involved, we thought it wise to organize them into heats, like swimmers: a glass heat, internal heat, and external heat. But unlike swimmers, who are judged based on speed, the toys would be assessed qualitatively. I suggested we use the criteria for judging rhythmic gymnastics: technical merit, artistic value, and execution.

Before we even got started, Erin expressed outrage over the pre-game performance of one of the contenders. The Talking Head Audio Enhanced Vibrator, a rabbit-style vibrator that talks dirty using sound chips, arrived broken.

"I'm so upset," she said. "I'm trying to get another one, because if I don't hear Jean-Philippe talking dirty to you, I just don't think France will be properly represented in the Olympics."

There was no time to replace it, but we were consoled by the fact that more than twenty toys were available.

"We're gonna need a Costco number of batteries," Erin noted. "And some ice for the swelling."

We met for a pre-game beer at Benny's Burritos. Normally I orgasm quickly, but drinking beer decreases my ability to come, putting all the toys at a slight disadvantage and making the games more challenging. Drinking would also numb any physical pain. Beer is the sports medicine of masturbation.

Erin arrived carrying a giant bag labeled "Sex Toys." She was obviously inebriated. "Feel how heavy this is," she said, handing me the bag.

The bag felt like it held three bowling balls.

"But no peeking!" she warned, taking a seat. "I got you a

present," she added, handing me a terrycloth, John McEnroe-style headband and a packet of "Horny Goat Weed."

"Oh no, this is like steroids," I said, reading the label. "I'm gonna get 'roid rage."

"It's called doping."

"It claims to increase blood flow to the genitals. Is this going to give me a stroke?"

"No," reassured Erin, "I think I've taken it before."

Washing down my performance enhancer, I suggested we pick up some vegetables for a "produce heat," because before people had Pocket Rockets they were forced to make do with zucchini.

We'd barely been at the bar ten minutes when Erin began revealing the contents of her bag to everyone there. Whipping out the Talking Head Audio Enhanced Vibrator, she explained that the audio base had become detached from the vibrator, which no longer vibrated. But the good news was the sound chips still worked. A group of curious bar patrons gathered around the vibrator like it was a transistor radio during a blackout. Erin played the prerecorded fantasy scenarios, which included "Slow Ride with Koby," "Juan, the Latin Lover," and "Jean-Philippe, French Boy."

"Wow, Jean-Philippe's voice is so hot, I could listen to that all day," I said.

Others agreed that Jean-Philippe made their panties wet and wanted to hear more, but after two beers, it was time to hit the vegetable stand. On our way out, bar-goers wished my vagina good luck.

All Olympic games have a motto, and ours was "Beggars Can't Be Choosers." Not only were we limited to what we could get for free, the vegetable selection at the local bodega was abysmal.

"Ew, we are really gonna have to scrub these," I noted, picking up a dirty-yet-phallic yam and taking it to the checkout along with a cucumber, zucchini, and carrot. Because we were only buying phallic vegetables and no lettuce or dressing, I was certain everyone knew what we were up to. Just in case they didn't, Erin announced to the store, "We're going to put these in her vagina!" For emphasis, she pointed toward my crotch.

Erin showed her giant bag of sex toys to everyone we passed, even a well-dressed couple sitting at an outdoor café sharing a bottle of wine.

"Feel how heavy this is," she said, handing the man her bag.

"That *is* heavy," he said.

"Yep. It's gonna be a long night."

Back at my crib, Erin emptied the contents of her bag onto my bedspread. It looked we'd just held up the Pink Pussycat Boutique. She gave a brief commentary on each toy. "This was made by women for women," she said, pointing to a Magnifique Natural Contours Vibrator.

"It looks like an at-home microdermabrasion kit," I said.

"This one is from Sweden," Erin noted, holding up a tiny Lily Vibrator in antique pink. "It costs $129." She then produced a bright yellow vibrator. "Here Germany is represented. This is the Dinky Digger."

"It looks like a mole, and it's holding a flower! Cute!"

"And it hits your G-spot like you would not believe."

"That's not going to get all the way in. It's too fat."

"That's what the lube is for," she said, pulling out a five-pack of Wet flavored lube and a bottle of *Pjur* German lube.

"*Klebt garantiert nicht* is now the only German phrase I know. It means 'guaranteed never sticky.'"

I suggested we engage in a blind taste test of the flavored lubes.

Erin poured a drop of each flavor on her fingers, which I then licked with my eyes closed, attempting to identify the flavors. Amazingly, the lube engineers at Wet have managed to perfectly replicate the flavor of piña coladas. The only unidentifiable flavor was "passion fruit," which tasted just like Hi-C.

The largest heat was the glass heat, which featured six dildos in all, two of which were hand-blown by a dude who fabricates bongs. Glass, Erin noted, is all the rage because you can heat it up and cool it down.

As she spoke, vibrators buzzed all over the bed.

"Which ones are visually sexy to you?" Erin asked.

"Well, I'll tell you what's not sexy: the Dinky Digger," I said. "It looks like something out of *Yellow Submarine*. The glass ones *look* the sexiest. That one is cute," I said, pointing to a small vibe with a bear-shaped clitoral stimulator.

"Which ones scare you?"

"These two," I said, straining to lift two massive glass dildos. "They weigh about fifty pounds each. Any sex toy that reminds me of a discus is scary. And that tongue attachment that goes on the bullet vibe is scary in more of a *Silence of the Lambs* way."

"It made me come."

Commemorating the theft of fire from the Greek god Zeus by Prometheus, Erin lit the ceremonial torch—in this case, a very large joint. My room filled with more smoke than Spicoli's van as I splayed my legs and prepared my beaver for the external heat. A classic Pocket Rocket started the games and would have ended the games a few seconds later had Erin not replaced it with the more genteel Lily. The Lily's small size makes it great for traveling, and though it's not as direct as the Pocket Rocket, it works on a slow build. Unfortunately, it doesn't cover a lot of area. Once you put it down on the bed it's easily lost, especially if you own twenty other toys. The Natural Contours vibe was thrust upon me next, but I wasn't sure where it should go or to what natural contours it was supposed to conform.

Erin grew visibly weary as I barked commands like a bitchy choreographer: "Move it up. Move it down. To the left. To the right."

Frustrated, she swapped Natural Contours for the bullet vibe with the creepy tongue attachment. It felt like something one might accidentally step on in the ocean: soft and slimy. Erin tried a combo, pressing the tiny Lily against my clit while thrusting the slimy fake tongue against my vaginal opening. This combo worked wonders but didn't push me over the edge.

I wanted to use my fingers to finish myself off, but that would have clouded my judgment of the vibrators. As my head swooned, the vibrator with the honey bear clitoral stimulator was thrust against me. The bear only had one setting: high.

Greedily, I snatched it from my lab partner and thrust it inside myself. This was technically cheating because we were still in the external heat, but when you're seconds away from coming, cheating is an option. I worked the little vibrator in and out until I came.

Emerging from my postorgasmic haze, I felt something gooey. The entire bottle of passion fruit lube had leaked on my bed. We were swimming in it. My room smelled like a punch bowl.

Removing the soiled comforter, we began the internal heat. Again, combos worked best. I held the Lily to my clit while trying out the bigger fellas, including the pasty penis and red, satanic-looking dildo. I eyed the Dinky Digger, whose silliness was starting to charm me despite his girth. But the time was right; I was lubed up with natural juices and passion fruit spillage.

Erin slicked up the little fellow and slowly inserted him. His curved, smiling head greeted my g-spot. As he ventured further inside, the flower in his hand stimulated my fleshy walls. Erin fiddled with the Dinky Digger's speed settings while I enjoyed his silicone surface, which felt smooth as skin. It didn't take long for the enchanted creature to produce a cascade of love juice. Plus, he was totally quiet—a bonus if you're not drowning out your vibrator with music.

Exhausted from only two rounds and two big Os, we took a beer/dildo-cleaning/peeing halftime break. Erin put the prettiest glass dildo, which featured a kaleidoscopic image of a flower, in the freezer.

"Don't forget it's in there," I warned her. "I don't think my roommate wants to discover that when he reaches for frozen tamales."

The second half of the games proved a disappointment. The freezer dildo was too cold, causing the tongue-to-frozen-flagpole effect. My body was weary. The red sea was unwilling to part, even for more sex toys. It was a scoreless overtime, and Erin and I were both ready to call it a night.

The next day, Erin said her arm was so tired she felt like she'd just pitched nine innings. My vagina was worn out. Worst of all, I wasn't sure which toy should win. If I were stranded on a desert island, I'd want a toy that offered the most options. By those standards, the Talking Vibrator would be my first choice. It offers the greatest variety of speed settings, a clitoral stimulator, and a penis head that swivels. Plus, it speaks French. Sadly, it was disqualified. To make up my mind, I masturbated a few more times, but my clit still had a hard time deciding. I even tried a wearable vibrator, figuring I could get my errands done while testing it out. But the leg straps irritated my thighs, and it looked as subtle under clothing as heavy-duty adult diapers. Maybe I'm as picky as Goldilocks, but I think the perfect sex toy has yet to be invented.

I used the Lily more than the others, but mostly in an assistive role, kind of like a wing to a striker. And I'm not sure any vibrator is worth $129. As for technical merit, the Pocket Rocket wins for speed and efficiency. But aesthetically, it leaves a lot to be desired. The Dinky Digger, on the other hand, has both technical and artistic merit, and it executes orgasms with finesse, despite its oafishness.

So it was the little mole from Germany that took the gold, followed by the Swedish Lily in second place and the Japanese Pocket Rocket in third. The most shocking result of the Sex Toy Olympics is that once they were done, I was tired of masturbating. Give me four years, I thought, and I might feel differently.

27

GETTING METAPHYSICAL

I SWUNG BY Nerve's office to drop off pictures of the sex toys wearing little penis-emblazoned Olympic medals. Standing opposite Ada's desk, I filled her in on my descent into monogamy.

"Wow. He's hot," she said.

"I know, but I don't know what to do about the column."

Daniel wasn't like my other "lab partners." He was private, a little shy, and a romantic who would most likely not be willing to wear vibrating condoms or cockrings for the sake of journalism.

When I told him about my past experiments a look of mild horror crossed his face.

"Weren't you afraid you might catch something?" he asked when I described the orgy.

A man who gets busy at an orgy will get high fives, whereas a woman might get little more than a dirty look. Sexually experienced men are viewed as Casanovas, whereas I ran the risk of being seen as a hardened slut. Rationally, I knew it was a double standard perpetuated by the patriarchy to keep all the Madonnas from becoming whores. Yet neurotically I wondered: had I become a skank?

I reflected on my year. I'd partied like a rock star—boozed with metal bands, engaged in a four-way, smoked opium, and eaten giant cheese balls. Although it had been fun, it had been spiritually empty.

It was clearly time for a little stroll down the path to enlightenment. I felt like Pattie Boyd on the eve of her Maharishi Mahesh Yogi phase. But the thought of giving up sex and alcohol did not appeal to me, especially now that I had a boyfriend so hot he made my yoni flow like the Ganges River. Luckily, there is tantra—the self-improvement rite one can engage in while naked and boning.

I wondered if it was really better than regular sex. It is mostly hippies who espouse the virtues of tantric sex, and I have always been mistrustful of hippies, the result of reading *Helter Skelter* during my formative years. There was only one way to find out.

I breathed a sigh of relief when Daniel agreed to try it on two conditions: anonymity and the freedom to forgo workshops.

"Tantra actually sounds kind of hot," he said. "But what exactly is it?"

"I have no idea," I said. "When I find out, we'll try out everything I've learned."

Though Daniel refused to take part in embarrassing classes, I was still free to humiliate myself. Online I found a class called "Cultivating Self-Love through Tantra" and signed up.

Because class was still a few days off, I embarked on some

research. At Babeland, I rented two instructional DVDs and bought a book called *Tantric Sex: Learn the Ancient Art of Eastern Lovemaking.*

At home, I popped in the first DVD, *Tantric Guide to Sexual Potency.* It cut between a redheaded hippie woman talking and shots of various couples banging away. At one point, one of the actors pulled his "wand of light" out of an actress's vag and spooged on her ass. The difference between this and regular porn eluded me. Tom stopped by and also was baffled.

"It's like a regular porno with a voiceover," he noted.

"I think it's supposed to be tantric because they're making 'deep' faces instead of regular porn faces," I said.

Perturbed, I turned off the TV just as Bruce dropped by.

"How bad could it be?" he asked. "As bad as the female ejaculation video we watched?"

"It made the female ejaculation video look like *Citizen Kane*," I said. "And I still have no idea what tantra is."

"I think its like fucking for hours without thrusting," Bruce suggested.

"Hours of fucking without thrusting, and you're dating a twenty-six-year-old dude?" Tom asked. "Good luck, Rev."

Undeterred, I put on *Hearts Cracked Open*, a DVD about lesbian tantra. The women describe tantra in a variety of ways: a tool for making relationships better, a way of cultivating your spirit, and a method for achieving altered states of consciousness. Since I am about one acid tab away from a Syd Barrett–style freakout, the idea of achieving altered states sans chemicals appeals to me.

Next, I studied the book *Tantric Sex* by Suzie Hayman, which includes wacky photos of couples cavorting. The text briefly summarizes tantra's 5,000-year history, teaches vocab terms like *kundalini* (life force energy), *soul-gazing* (staring into each other's eyes), and *lingam* (penis), while offering suggestions on tantric room décor (candles, colorful fabric, and pillows). Ms. Hayman outlines steps for the tantric love-making ritual: bathe each other, dance for each other, massage each other, and feed each other fruit. Basically, be really nice to whomever you're about to fuck.

Still, when she covers fucking, she just lists all of the positions people use anyway but refers to them with fancy names. For instance, oral sex is referred to as "mouth congress." One novel suggestion the author proposes is to make a "pair of tongs," wherein the female gets on top and grips her partner's lingam with her yoni muscles.

A few days later, I attended the workshop.

It was held at a midtown rehearsal space crawling with theater majors. Kundalini burst forth from jazz hands; a cacophony of Broadway show tunes assaulted me from every angle. I felt like bashful Doris Finsecker awaiting her audition in *Fame*.

Eventually, my sole classmate arrived. She was a normal-looking woman named Janelle. We were escorted to a studio where our instructor, Shakti Cheryll, greeted us. Wasting no time, she popped a CD into her boom box and began doing interpretive dance.

"This is kind of primal," she said, turning up the New Age music to drown out the students singing the body electric next door.

"Plant your feet firmly on the ground. Imagine you have roots like a tree," she instructed. "And just feel the music. Let your body move to it."

Though I felt like a moron, I visualized roots growing into my tired feet and imagined being a warrior tree in *Lord of the Rings*.

After dancing and doing guttural breathing exercises, we sat cross-legged on the floor as our teacher gave us an overview of the philosophies of tantra. Realizing very little of it was about sex, and feeling tired from the previous night of debauchery, I began to zone out.

When she announced it was time to meditate and that we could do so while lying down, I thought finally I would get some rest. Lying on the floor with my palms turned toward the ceiling, I focused on Shakti Cheryll's soft voice. As she told me I was walking through a field of flowers, I pictured marigolds and imagined their scent. She instructed us to leave the field of flowers and walk through a wooded area before coming to a pond.

"I want you to think of a time when you felt love," she murmured, "and immerse yourself in the pond."

As I sat in the pond, a barrage of images assailed me, but one memory continually emerged: JJ, deathly ill as a puppy. Remembering the day she got out of the animal hospital, I recalled how happy our reunion had been. It was embarrassing—all the lovers I've had and people I've cared about, and I couldn't help thinking about my dog. Silly as it felt, I didn't fight it. I imagined holding her tiny body and crying tears of relief into her fur. Soon real tears were flowing down my cheeks, making me feel even more foolish, until I heard Janelle crying, too.

After we emerged from our meditation, we analyzed what we'd seen and felt. I told my teacher that JJ has given me what no human has: the ability to love unconditionally without fear of being hurt. My love for her is maternal and uncomplicated.

Before we left, Shakti Cheryll told us that the love we'd felt while chilling in our imaginary ponds was real. She put her hand over her heart chakra. "It's right here," she said, "and you can go to it whenever you need to."

Thanking her, I bolted from the studio. One of the reasons I've avoided self-improvement is that self-improvement is for people with time on their hands, and I have no time on my hands. I still had no idea what tantric sex was, and I needed to find out fast. Daniel was coming over the following night.

I traipsed up to a midtown Barnes and Noble, where I found just what I'd been looking for: *The Complete Idiot's Guide to Tantric Sex* by Dr. Judy Kuriansky. Purchasing anything with the words "idiot" and "sex" in the title is mortifying. Feeling slightly less cool than the time I purchased an English-to-Elvish glossary, I placed the book face down on the counter at checkout. The salesperson flipped it over, and I was certain every customer in the store was pointing and laughing at me.

But it was I who got the last laugh, because *The Complete Idiot's Guide to Tantric Sex* is a tome bursting with insight.

Tantra, Dr. Kuriansky explains, is a Sanskrit word meaning "the teachings and practices that use energy to lead to a high state of bliss and enlightenment." Tantric sex is when you apply these teachings to boning. The guide then goes on to explain how to do this using bulleted lists, outlines, writing exercises, and quizzes.

Chapter 5, "Honoring the God and Goddess in You," explains that in tantric sex, partners honor each other the way they would revered beings. It then lists well-known gods and goddesses and asks readers to list their own along with the admirable qualities they embody. Among my goddesses were Pippi Longstocking (strength) and Cher (power). My gods were Keith Richards (immortality) and SpongeBob (fun).

Once I'd finished listing deities and doing a series of pelvic thrusts, I focused on Chapter 12, which had detailed illustrations and advice on massage and "lingam pleasuring." If tantric sex meant honoring my partner as I would a god, I would do just that.

At eight o'clock the next night, Daniel arrived. Because we were too nervous to strip naked immediately and make like Shiva and Shakti, we took a bottle of wine up to my roof, where I gave him a rundown on what I'd learned.

"I'm sorry," I said. "I know it's cheesy."

"Jen, you know that no matter how goofy it is, I'll go at it with total sincerity," he said. "Just one thing: when you say the word 'yoni,' it makes me think of Yanni, and it makes me go soft."

"We won't mention Yanni or anything that connotes Yanni," I promised.

Determined not to half-ass it, we practiced soul gazing, breathing techniques, and touching each other's chakra zones. Chakra-touching led to kissing, which led to Daniel's lingam throbbing against his trousers.

It was time to go downstairs to the tantric temple and get busy. Candles were lit, a *Reiki Forest* CD cranked, and, just in time for our first tantric encounter, a wild thunderstorm began. Fully clothed, we parked ourselves in yab yum—Daniel cross-legged with me straddling his lap. We synchronized our breathing and soul-gazed before moving on to the next step. Though both books recommended bathing each other as part of the ritual, we skipped this step since my shower is in a closet in my kitchen, and my roommate could walk in at any second. Instead I offered him a massage.

We stripped, and he lay on his stomach. After warming oil between my hands, I ran my fingers up and down his body, from his calves to his back. Turning over, he lay on his back, propping up pillows so he could watch, as Dr. Kuriansky suggested. *The Idiot's Guide* also cautioned that as a man lies on his back, a traditionally "female" passive position, he might feel vulnerable. As if on cue, Daniel announced, "I have never felt more vulnerable in my life."

I assured him that all he had to do was relax. He didn't have to worry about staying hard or accidentally jizzing on his masseuse's hands. Like me, tantra is not goal-oriented.

"Just enjoy yourself," I said, lubing him up and taking him between my palms. The act of stroking a penis with no intent of getting its owner off was unfamiliar, but liberating. I had to remind myself that I wasn't giving a hand job, but a lingam massage. The goal was not to choke the chicken, but to pet the chicken and basically give the chicken the best night of its life.

Because I'm a perfectionist, I'd studied the section on lingam massage the way a Harvard law student might study for the bar exam. Still, I worried it might seem too clinical, like playing doctor, so I made a point of looking into Daniel's eyes as I "palmed his crown" and "polished his helmet." When I placed one hand around the base and used the other to work the tip like an orange juicer it appeared he was ready to explode. I languished over his lingam until he was so turned on he suggested I hop on board.

Straddling him, I slipped my dripping yoni onto his wand. Rain blew through the window onto our skin. He used his free hands to caress my skin and polish my pearl until I nearly blacked out from pleasure. Opening my eyes, we kissed and soul-gazed. Leaning back, I used the "pair of tongs" to squeeze his lingam like a hot piece of pound cake. Rocking back and forth, I put my hand over his heart chakra.

"Put your hand on my heart," I said. He stretched his hand out and placed it on my chest. His energy raced through me like electricity. It was similar to the scene in *The Dark Crystal* where the Gelflings share all of their memories and experiences, just by touching hands.

Up to this point, I'd doubted the veracity of tantric sex. I'd thought maybe it was a 5,000-year-old hoax perpetuated by hippies out to make a buck off premature ejaculators. But when Daniel touched my heart, I felt the love he had for me as a human being, and I understood why tantric sex will be here long after bukkake and rainbow parties have gone. It's not about clits, titties, ass, boners, or even sucking your jizz back up your spine and into the coiled serpent lying dormant within you. It's about consciously feeling your own energy and giving it to your lover while you also give that person your body.

Daniel must have felt this too, because we gave ourselves over to the apparent cheesiness with abandon.

"You look so beautiful right now. It's like I'm fucking nature," he said.

"You look so beautiful," I said. "I feel like I'm fucking Hercules. But not the Kevin Sorbo Hercules, more like the one I imagined."

He looked at me with so much reverence I felt like Cher, Aphrodite, Galadriel, and Demeter rolled into one. It was hard to believe we were still in a tenement on the Lower East Side. I half expected Pegasus to circle above my bed.

Blissed out, we continued slowly flopping around on my bed in a dizzying display of positions, mindfully soul-gazing and breathing together. When we did pick up the pace, Daniel had to pull out a few times so as not to blow his load. At one point we took a break, drank Budweiser, and ate chocolate. (My research uncovered several methods for delaying orgasm, and though none of them mentioned Budweiser, "taking a break" was suggested.)

I replaced the *Reiki* CD with a homemade playlist, full of music infused with mystical imagery: T. Rex, the Beatles, and the Zombies.

After going to "mouth congress" on his penis, we were ready for another ecstatic union. His love arrow vibrated inside me, and I knew it was only a matter of time until he reached the point of no return.

"What do you want, Jen?" he asked.

"I think it's probably time you fucked me as hard and fast as you want," I answered, pulling my knees to my chest.

As the late George Harrison's melodious voice echoed forth from my laptop, I completely understood, singing my own inspired chant. "My, my, my Lord . . . oh my God . . . don't stop," I moaned, pulling Daniel closer.

"Are you sure?"

"Uh huh."

"Okay."

Moments later he came, filling a condom with enough seminal fluid to irrigate a small village.

"Wow. Crown condoms are durable," I noted as he slid the sheath from his lingam. "That was incredible."

"Amazing."

"You know what's weird?" I remarked. "I have no idea how long we were at it."

Because clocks are not part of tantric home décor, I'd turned mine toward the wall. Flipping it back toward me, I was startled.

"It's 2 AM!" I exclaimed. "I thought it was, like, eleven or something."

It was as if we'd been in a time warp. We were far from tired; if anything, we had more energy. We dressed and headed out to a bar to celebrate our accomplished boning. This was probably a mistake, because the next day we had about as much vitality as the English Patient.

While I'll always enjoy the occasional bar-bathroom quickie, it can't beat whatever it is Daniel and I engaged in. I say "whatever it is" because I'm still not sure it was actually tantric sex. If tantric sex means languorously fucking in order to create, through touch, a psychic bond you thought only Gelflings were capable of, then we had tantric sex. And it rocked.

As Daniel later said, "I don't know what it was. Maybe it was somewhere in the middle of the lingam massage, but I think you touched my very soul."

Similarly, I felt the core of my being had been touched and cherished. And amazingly, this hadn't interfered with the jackability of the experience. It only made it hotter.

If you ever left the womb, you've probably had your heart broken. But tantra gives you the freedom to behave as if you've never been hurt before. There was an innocence to the tantric ritual that I hadn't experienced since my first love. Tantric sex challenged me to be totally open and to let my Daniel inside my head and heart. While few things are more terrifying, the reward—discovering a little magic still exists—was worth it.

28   SPACE

DANIEL FREAKED OUT when the tantric sex article appeared. Even though I'd given him a pseudonym, people knew we were dating. Men and women he barely knew were suddenly asking him how his lingam was hanging.

He felt hurt because he thought I'd revealed too much. I felt hurt because revealing too much is what I do, and he knew that the moment he put his lingam into my yoni.

"It's not that I didn't think it was a great article; it was. It's just that I don't think I can be part of your column."

This left me with two options: give up writing about him or lose him. It was my art or my man. I knew that if I couldn't write about him and I couldn't fuck other people, my column would get the ax. There are only so many stories one can write about masturbation.

My whole life I'd chosen art over love. *I'd chosen art over everything.* As a result, I had no semblance of a normal life. And being a sex columnist made my already crazy life crazier. I was tired of it. I wanted to have sex for the sake of sex again. After all the wild experiments I'd tried, all I really wanted was to lie down in bed and fuck the man I loved. I'd done so much weird shit that a penis and a bed seemed like a novelty.

So, for the first time in my life, I chose love over art.

As expected, the column got canned. Ada and Michael said it had "run its course" and asked me if I wanted to write one final installment, to end with a bang. I didn't. I wanted to relax. I felt like a prostitute who'd been freed from her pimp.

The fact that I was now broke hardly mattered because I had Daniel, and together, we had New York City in the summer. We rode the Cyclone twice in a row, drank beer on the Coney Island boardwalk, went for walks with no destination, spent hours sitting in the sunlight doing nothing, made out on every floor of the Whitney Museum, and climbed trees in Central Park. We were the type of happy couple I would have previously rolled my eyes at.

We made love from dusk till dawn. I poured all of the love in my chest into his chest and all of the thoughts in my head into his head until everything else faded away. I couldn't tell where my skin ended and his began. I forgot that I had skin, or hands or legs or anything but energy. It was as if a portal opened up and we could climb through and experience pure bliss.

"You're like an ambassador to the other world," he said to me as we lay in bed bathed in sweat and female ejaculate. "You're so magical you should have a unicorn horn growing out of your head."

Even when the weather got cold, our romance continued. We went on dates like normal people. One night in

November, we went to the Metropolitan Museum of Art and held hands as we looked at art. I'd been a guard there a decade earlier. Clothed in a heinous polyester uniform, I'd been forced to stand still while happy couples kissed in front of the paintings as a prelude to de-pantsing each other at home. Now I was in a happy couple relationship. I beamed with joy and pride.

We lay down on a bench in front of Picasso's *Gertrude Stein* and kissed.

"I just want to feel you kiss my cheek forever," Daniel said.

And I wanted to kiss his cheek forever.

Forever, as it turns out, is forty-eight hours in dude years. Because two days later, Daniel dumped me.

"I just can't do this anymore. I need some space," he said.

I can't do this anymore, I need some space is code for "You're not the one." Daniel was a romantic. He believed in *the one*. I believed in the moment and hadn't realized the moment might end.

"Don't you like being with me?" I asked.

"I love being with you."

"Don't you like making love to me?"

"Yes. YES. But you just don't get it. My life is a mess, and I can't be with you and get it together. It's going to get bad, and I don't want to hurt you."

"But you ARE hurting me! Right now. YOU are hurting ME. If your life is a mess, why am I the part that has to go? What about pot or booze? Am I just a bad fucking habit that you have to kick?"

"No. It's not like that. Jen, it's not about you."

It's not about you is the last thing any dumpee wants to

hear because when you're a dumpee, you know damn well that it *is* about you because *you* have just been rejected. Even if the dumper tells you they're dumping you so they can find themselves. Even if they are dumping you to move to Alaska and work on a fishing vessel. Even if they are leaving you for rehab or they're joining AA and they can't look at you without wanting a drink. Even if they shave their head and tell you they're dumping you so they can join a cult. Even if they dump you for a model. Even if they dump you to be alone. They have just dumped you, and no matter how you slice it and dice it, it's a rejection of *you*—your mind, body, and heart.

It's saying: *Can we still be friends, because I don't think I EVER WANT TO HAVE SEX WITH YOU AGAIN.* It's saying: *Remember that awesome blowjob you gave me last week? I don't want one of those EVER AGAIN.* It's saying: *Remember all of those great nights when we sat on your roof and looked at the stars and had so much fun? I NEVER WANT TO DO THAT WITH YOU AGAIN. You know your vagina? I never want to see it again. Your penis? I never want to see it again. Your eyes? I never want to look into them again. Your lips? I never want to kiss them again. Yes, I want to still be your friend, but you are not good enough for me for whatever reason, so I'm throwing you out like the used condom I filled with seminal fluid after penetrating your vagina last Tuesday.*

This kind of rejection is known as heartache.

"It *is* about me," I said. "*I* am the one sitting here crying. *I* am the one with the broken heart."

"Maybe I'm making the worst mistake of my life," he said, burying his head in his hands.

I sat on his lap and put my arms around him, crying. I

tried to imagine my heart chakra glowing and pressed my chest to his like we did when we made love. He pressed his nose to mine, and I stared into his light green eyes. My reflection stared back.

"Wow, I can see myself in your eyes," he said.

"Me too."

My heart was broken. In my life I'd been dumped, betrayed, rejected, and tormented, and I'd done all of those things to others. But I'd never been dumped by someone who still loved me. I thought of how I'd dumped Dog years ago and realized Daniel was doing the same thing to me. And I knew the pain he would eventually feel would be much greater than my own.

Thoughts of him destroyed with regret ten years down the line did little to soothe my broken heart. And since I no longer had the extra income from my column, I was now broke as well as heartbroken. Carrie on *Sex and the City* got to buy Manolo Blahniks any time she had her heart broken. I couldn't do that.

So I tried to do drugs. A friend gave me a box of pot cookies. I ate one, got the munchies, and ate the rest. Then I thought I was dying and had to call an EMT, who diagnosed me as being "really stoned."

So drugs were out. Shopping was out. Because I didn't want to wake up three months later with a burning vagina and a roster of stalkers, anonymous sex was out.

The only thing I could do was wait for the pain to go away.

I marked off days on the calendar, drank Budweiser, and listened exclusively to tragic country music while wearing the extra-large wifebeater Daniel had left draped over my door. It held the last vestiges of his scent along with a tiny marijuana burn hole over the left breast. Inhaling the fabric deeply, I longed for some kind of Proustian reverie of his big and tall body wrapped around mine. Instead it seemed everything reminded me of his absence and the space now surrounding me. It was the space Daniel insisted he wanted: the vast, cold, empty space outside of my hot, pink, tight, nurturing, squirting, multiorgasmic vagina that had never asked him for a fucking thing.

Because the Lower East Side is a small town and because Daniel and I are both borderline alcoholics, it wasn't long before we ran into each other at a party, got drunk, and fucked. This led to more fucking coupled with romantic dates, and I entered a delusional state wherein I believed he had let me back into his heart. But I knew pain was on the horizon. I was learning to sense heartache the way elephants can sense a tsunami.

We were invited to a friend's wedding in the Catskills, which I saw as an opportunity for a romantic getaway, and which Daniel saw as the perfect opportunity to dump me one final time. As we stood under a rainbow surrounded by mountains, he hit me with one last cliché: He "loved" me but he was not "in love" with me.

At this point I wasn't sure I was "in love" with him either, but I didn't see why that should interfere with us "fucking for hours."

With the open bar in close proximity, I downed several Budweisers and wandered into the dark forest in five-inch heels. Moments later I found myself splayed on my back at the bottom of a ditch. For a minute I thought about taking a nap, but a concerned wedding attendee noticed me there and lent me a hand.

I emerged from this indignity with a lump the size of a baseball on my coccyx.

"Maybe you're finally growing the tail you always wanted," said my friend George.

Tom, Faceboy, and Bruce, who were all at the wedding, tried to console me. Tom and his date hung a "Just Hang in There" kitten postcard on my hotel room door. But even baby animals weren't helping.

It hurt to walk. It hurt to sit. It hurt to lie down. But even worse than the pain in my ass was the pain in my heart. The following day when I returned to the city, I had a nervous breakdown.

It started as a panic attack. A panic attack is basically what happens when your fight-or-flight reflex acts as though you've just met a bear in the woods, even though you're sitting in front of your computer eating a sandwich. I'd had a couple of panic attacks before, mainly after my botched appendectomy, which I covered in the first chapter. Those panic attacks lasted for only a few minutes, but this one lasted for almost two hours. Convinced I was having a stroke, I lay in my roommate's bed with my feet elevated and commanded him to call 911. Maybe my EMT friends from the pot-smoking episode would pick up. When the police showed up instead of an ambulance, it began to dawn on me that they had come to "take me away."

"Where are the doctors?" I asked, my panic doubling in severity.

"You're not having a stroke," the policemen said.

Finally, two EMTs did arrive, only to complain about my sixth-floor walkup. They assured me I wasn't dying even though my heartbeat was up to 180.

"Do you want to go with us?" they asked, according to protocol.

I knew they wouldn't take me anywhere nice like Promises, but instead to a terrifying city hospital where they would drug and abuse me.

"No."

"Are you sure?"

"Yes."

"Okay, well if you call again we're *going* to take you," they threatened, then turned and left.

Armed with the knowledge that if I went insane again I would be institutionalized, I decided that, for the first time in my life, it might be time to try therapy.

Problem was I couldn't afford therapy. Instead, I spent entire days on the phone with Faceboy.

"I just want to drink coffee again," I said.

"You will. Trust me."

"And alcohol."

"You will."

I missed coffee and beer. I wake up *in order* to drink coffee and beer, and now my nerves were so shot, I couldn't drink either. Something had to be done. As I lay in my sickbed perusing the *Village Voice*, an ad popped out at me: *Do you suffer from panic attacks?* Test subjects were needed for a study at Columbia University. The payment: three hundred bucks and six months of free therapy. Frantically, I dialed the number.

A guard at the front desk gave me a sticker that said "New York Psychiatric Hospital Visitor." *Now everyone knows I'm insane*, I thought, affixing it to my jacket. He then directed me to the fourth floor, where a kindly admin named Brendan handed me a stack of forms containing questions about my

mental health, family history, and lifestyle. As I checked off
the variety of substances I've put into my body throughout
the years, I wondered how I'd managed to stave off a trip to
the psych ward for so long.

I met with the psychiatrist in charge of the study. After
talking to me for half an hour, he diagnosed me as suffering
from panic disorder. He also told me it's not unusual for a
person to develop this disorder after an emotional upheaval,
specifically a loss or a breakup. I told him about the injuries
to my ass and my heart.

Finally I was given a series of blood tests, which revealed
that I was healthy enough to be a test subject along with
the even more shocking news that my liver is functioning
normally.

The study was broken down into two parts. I would
undergo both a PET scan and an MRI so that doctors could
look at my brain to try to determine why people have panic
attacks. I signed up.

For the PET scan, they inserted a catheter into an artery
on my wrist—not a walk in the park for someone suffering from a panic disorder. The doctors, aware of my fragile
mental state, handled me like a newborn baby chick. They
brought me lunch and hooked up a DVD player so I could
watch movies while they poked and prodded. I'd brought
along HBO's *Rome*, hoping a little gladiatorial man-ass
might quell my anxiety. It worked until the doctors injected
me with a radioactive compound that collected in my body
and began emitting nuclear gamma rays; the smell and taste
of it were horrifying, like a pen had exploded in my esopha-
gus and was leaking ink into my bloodstream. But terror soon
gave way to another emotion: sorrow. *What am I doing here?* I

wondered, remembering the fun sexperiments I'd tried in the past. Now I was a *real* guinea pig in an actual lab.

Tears rolled down my cheeks and onto the soft foam of the PET scan machine. It was the first time I'd cried since being dumped. I felt like the mythological nymph, Echo, after Narcissus dumped her (because he also needed space) and she lost her voice. I was a faint whisper of my former fun-loving self. The girl who'd once cavorted at orgies, danced at Wiggles, and plunged headfirst into a giant balloon half-naked in the name of science was gone. I *had* ended on a bang, but one more fitting a science fiction double feature than a sex column.

In the twisted experiment known as my life, a variable I'd never expected, but one that's not surprising given the amount of fucking involved, had occurred: I had fallen in love. This resulted in a horrible accident that obliterated both the guinea pig and scientist, leaving a naked blob of need, mental disorder, and heartbreak in their wake.

But I cannot end as a blob. Even *The Outer Limits* and *Star Trek* don't end with blobs. In science fiction, a poignant ending is required to justify all the explosions, mysterious fluids, and extraterrestrial beings that precede it. Hence something amazing must emerge from any mysterious blob.

After two months of therapy, the unemployed blob of need gurgling in the fetal position on my kitchen floor began to transform. The panic soon disappeared and I stopped hauling my ass all the way uptown for therapy. Instead I focused on painting. It was the one thing that got me through my existential angst-ridden teen years, and now it helped get me through my existential angst-ridden thirties. I hadn't painted in years, and now it was just flowing out of me. Most of the paintings depicted Jen Junior and me floating around on the astral plane. My friend Jason called them "an interior decorator's worst nightmare."

I had fully expected to be bitter and angry for pretty much the rest of my life for having taken a chance on love only to end up unemployed and in a psychiatric hospital. But I soon realized that having my heart broken was not the worst thing that could have happened to me. The space Daniel had insisted on giving me was now filled with art, and for that I felt nothing but gratitude.

Shakti Cheryll taught me a tantric aphorism, which I now understood: *That by which you fall is that by which you rise.* The person I'd become after two years of science and chaos was stronger than both the guinea pig and the scientist because I'd had the courage to love without fear. And I would probably do it again in a heartbeat.

EPILOGUE

SOMEONE ONCE SAID that the first goal of an artist is to find his or her voice and the second goal of an artist is to lose that voice. Otherwise you get stuck in a rut. If I hadn't fallen for Daniel, maybe I wouldn't be sitting here writing the epilogue for this book. Maybe I'd be sitting on a Stealth butt plug while wearing the latest hands-free vibrator and writing about that instead. (Maybe I *am* sitting on a butt plug . . .) Point is, if I were still writing about butt plugs, orgies, four-ways, vibrators, and everything in between, not only would I have an asshole the size of the Grand Canyon, I would be bored to tears. And avoiding boredom is still my singular goal in life.

I didn't want to be a sex columnist forever, partly because I now viewed sex differently. With Daniel I'd managed to reach a mystical state, and I wasn't sure I could swap soul-gazing for drunkenly inserting change into bar bathroom condom machines. But I also didn't want a boyfriend: someone who might inadvertently ruin my life or try to censor me. I just wanted a little magic, something outside of the everyday.

When you're used to seeing performers do things like drinking douche and lighting their penises on fire each week, finding anything outside of the everyday becomes a challenging task.

I wrote a letter to Anthony, since he lives in a magical realm he's never left known as 1973. Along with his response, addressed to "Darling, Delicious, Delightful Jen," he enclosed two trolls and a letter of introduction from the trolls themselves. Their names were Oliver and Twist. Even in letters, Anthony was certainly not ordinary, but he was 3,000 miles away, and I could barely afford a trip on the subway, much less airfare back to London.

Hence my search for something out of the ordinary was confined to New York, where I was having no luck. I had plenty of dates and sex, but I couldn't even seem to reach an orgasm, let alone an enlightened state. I was just too sad to come. It was an exhausting time for men on the Lower East Side, many of whom wasted perfectly good cunnilingus skill sets on me. Even the cache of sex toys I'd amassed as a columnist held no interest for me.

My G-spot retreated further inside me, weeping silent, frustrated tears of female ejaculate. I had stopped looking.

It was on a morning when I was definitely *not* looking that I stumbled upon it—a surprise in a world where I'd become certain none existed. I was repulsively hung over from the Anti-Slam the night before, the historic last show. Collective Unconscious had previously been bulldozed by real estate developers and the bar where I'd recently been hosting it was closing—a new victim of gentrification. Hazy onstage memories of covering naked art stars in whipped cream danced in my desperately aching head. I'd lost a piece of myself with the end of the Anti-Slam, and I was pretty sure that piece was my liver.

I was still wearing makeup I'd slept in along with pajama pants that barely cut it as real pants when I showed up at the Downtown Heliport for Kat's bachelorette party. She was about to marry her long-time BF, Jesse, and a friend of hers had given them a surprise helicopter ride over Manhattan.

I stood alongside Kat's friends and family holding up the U in a grouping of signs that spelled out, "WE LOVE U KAT AND JESSE," as the couple flew overhead. Among Kat's friends from her hometown, I noticed a lanky boy in his twenties with crazy hair, chiseled features, and aquamarine eyes. He looked like David Bowie in *Labyrinth*: clearly not of this world.

"Who is that?" I asked Kat's mom.

"That's Shane, Kat's friend from childhood."

"He's hot."

"He's a drummer."

"I'm trying to stay away from musicians."

"Well, he's very sweet."

I couldn't stop staring at him. He was of such rare beauty it was like seeing a unicorn. I was still gawking when he suddenly looked over at me. We studied each other. I felt like I'd known him for eons. It was the same sense of familiarity that led me to bone Dog within fifteen minutes of meeting him.

As the party continued away from the Heliport, Shane and I got to know each other. Over drinks, I suggested he pay a visit to the Troll Museum, which is code for, "I want to have sex with you." We exchanged numbers.

The day of the wedding I woke up early and went out to get a German language guide since I was scheduled to perform in Berlin in four days and the only German phrase I knew was *"Klebt garantiert nicht"* from the label on the Pjur lube bottle. While shopping, I got a call from Shane.

As I was talking to him, I looked across the street and there he was. He looked up and saw me. I ran across the street and hugged him.

"Do you want to come over?" I asked him.

"Sure."

Back at my pad, he lounged on my bed as I decided what to wear, finally settling on a silver and pink mini-dress. I told him Moby (the pop star, whom Kat and I'd just made a video for) was supposed to be my platonic date, but that he'd cancelled the night before.

"Well, I know I'm not a famous musician, but perhaps I could be your new date," Shane said.

I accepted, frantically dialing Faceboy the moment Shane left to get changed for the wedding.

"Oh my God, Face, you should see Kat's childhood friend. He's so beautiful and he's gonna be my date tonight!" I was exploding with joie de vivre.

"Let's just pray that the horrible, tragic event of falling in love does not occur."

"He lives in California so I don't think there's much risk."

"In that case, I hope you get laid. I *want* you to get laid. In fact, if I have to pick his penis up and put it inside you I will."

"Thanks, Face."

Considering the way the last wedding I'd attended had gone, my expectations were very low. As long as I could escape without needing x-rays or therapy, I would be satisfied.

Shane arrived at the wedding wearing a black Beatles jacket, black pants, a pink shirt, and silver tie. He'd gotten the shirt and tie just to go with my outfit after he'd said goodbye. He'd even had the pink shirt pressed.

The attending art stars—Tanya, Tom, Michelle, and others—were impressed. I did my duty as bridesmaid and stood throughout the ceremony, which was followed by dinner and performances by a fire-eater and trapeze artists.

Afterward, Shane and I snuck outside and kissed. When we returned an hour had somehow passed and it was time for the after-party. We hopped in a car with a few art stars and sped off to Kat and Jesse's loft in Williamsburg. Once there, Shane and I made a detour and walked to the waterfront. It smelled rancid.

"It's nice being out in nature," I said, pointing to the one tree and the filthy water.

"Jen, you don't actually consider this nature, do you?"

"Yeah."

"You really must come out to California."

Inside, the party was bedlam. Kat and Jesse had a total of twelve exes there, which meant there were a number of guests crying. An inexperienced girl had been given acid for the first time and was hugging a wall, then making out with Kat's friend, Jeff, whose entire face was pierced and who'd been arrested at the airport on his way to the wedding for carrying a knife. There was a sword-swallower, confetti cannon, tango dancers, two fistfights, and a person in a tux passed out on the roof. It was the last party held at Kat and Jesse's loft, since the building was scheduled for demolition a week later—another victim of gentrification.

Eventually Shane and I left the party and headed back to the Troll Museum, where I offered him a piece of a pot cookie, which I'd been warned was exceedingly strong. A few bites later, we were stoned out of our minds and under a spell: wildly venturing completely into the Otherworld. We lay on my bed under a canopy of butterflies I'd painted on the ceiling, kissing and fucking, a web of enchantment and official New York City condoms growing around us. Our skin, breath, and minds melded into one.

I wasn't sure if we were actually opening our mouths to speak, or if we were speaking telepathically, but I asked him if this felt familiar and he said it did. When I straddled him and looked in his eyes, I saw all of the lovers I've ever had, past and future. Then he suddenly changed back into himself and we went back to the present. Then we went back to the past again. I kept thinking we were in the middle of a field and then I'd remember we were in my room.

"You came from the faerie realm, didn't you?" I asked.

"I think we're in the faerie realm," he said, touching my elf ears.

Maybe the pot cookie was talking or maybe I was overly affected by a recent rereading of *The Mists of Avalon*, but he appeared to be a magical creature. He touched my body in a manner that was healing and dirty, kissing my feet while my legs were at a ninety-degree angle to my body and he was penetrating me. And he never took his eyes off me. My heart chakra glowed as if he'd managed to fuck the sorrow right out of me and finally I was able to orgasm ... again and again. The floodgates of my urethral sponge opened while my broken heart vanished as quickly as it had appeared.

For forty-eight hours we went nuts, smoking weed, drinking, screwing, and listening to music. I discovered Shane was a Leo like me.

"Leos should really only ever fuck other Leos," I said, "My problem is that I've been fucking all of these air and water signs. They suck."

"They're all flakey."

It was very likely that all of my problems boiled down to bad astrological choices.

We took a shower together and he said, "I've never been able to shower with a woman because no one else likes it as hot as I do."

"I do," I said, soaping up his perfect penis until it was so clean I could see myself in it. "I like it so hot it hurts."

After more debauchery, showers, and one missed plane, he finally kissed me goodbye and left for California, while I left for Germany. We didn't exchange addresses. There was no reason to ruin such an incredible experience by staying in touch. I didn't feel sadness, only gratitude that the universe brought us together when it did.

I used to think nothing could beat first love, where you've never been hurt before and you're completely open. But now I think that love that comes along when you have been hurt, love that heals you, is pretty extraordinary, too, even if it's only for a weekend.

Lest readers think that my hopeful change of tone in this epilogue means I am dating again, this is not the case. I have still not read *The Rules*, nor do I want to. I'm not looking for Mr. Right or anyone to try to save me from my existence of bohemian extremism. I'm pretty sure my life partners are the art stars—my crazy friends who've been with me through thick and thin, circumcised and uncircumcised, flaccid and firm.

They've always been there for me and hopefully I'll always be here for them—in the squalid tenement I currently share with Reverend Jen Junior, two gay roommates, 400 trolls, and a handful of memories not suitable for my grandkids. I can't think of anyplace I'd rather be.

ACKNOWLEDGMENTS

I WOULD BE remiss if I did not mention the many individuals, real and imagined, who helped me survive the making of this book:

To my agent and friend, Jonathan Ames, thank you for having faith in the depraved and underachieving. To Anne Horowitz, Richard Nash, and everyone else at Soft Skull/Counterpoint. To my BFF, Faceboy, thank you for keeping me alive. Sorry about the phone bills. To my loyal protector and guardian angel, Reverend Jen Junior—thank you for existing. To Bruce Ronn, Kat Greene, Jason J-Boy Thompson, Tom Tenney, Robert Prichard, Courtney Webber, Monica Mohan, John Foster, Izzy, J.P., George Courtney, Moonshine, the Trachtenburgs, Velocity Chyaldd, Mangina, Amy, Bob, and Tobly, I offer my gratitude and love. To Dr. Sullivan, thank you for fixing my head. To Brid, thank you for listening to my prayers. To Nerve (especially Ada, Michael, and the photo editors who saw far too much of me each month) thanks for your encouragement and support. To my family, I thank you ahead of time for not disowning me. And to Si—I'm still waiting.